CLIMBING THE SYCAMORE TREE

CLIMBING THE SYCAMORE TREE

A STUDY ON CHOICE AND SIMPLICITY

Ann Hagmann

UPPER ROOM BOOKS®
NASHVILLE

Library of Congress Cataloging-in-Publication Data

Hagmann, Ann, 1948-
    Climbing the sycamore tree : a study on choice and simplicity / Ann Hagmann.
        p. cm.
    Includes bibliographical references.
    ISBN 0-8358-0946-3
1. Simplicity—Religious aspects—Christianity. 2. Christian life—Methodist authors. I. Title.

BV4647.S48 H34 2001
241'.68--dc21   2001017375

Printed in the United States of America on acid-free paper.

DEDICATION

To my Mother and Father
with gratitude and love

ACKNOWLEDGMENTS

I am grateful to the teachers and authors who have helped shape and form my thinking. The resources used in developing this workbook exposed me to "truth" and encouraged me to question "reality." I am forever in their debt. Also I would like to thank all those who participated in the testing of this study or offered editorial suggestions, especially Mary Brewington, who encouraged me to use my own voice. May each of you always be blessed with faith, hope, and love. I also thank the Upper Room Books editors—this book wouldn't be without them—George Donigian, who had faith in me and gave me a chance, JoAnn Miller for her overall direction, and Jeannie Crawford-Lee for her excellent editorial suggestions. Finally I thank God for my gifts of nature and nurture, for never giving up on me, and for enlightening me through the powerful presence of the holy Spirit and the sacred Scriptures.

This study is a faith witness
to God's presence with us
and God's love for us.

CONTENTS

PREVIEW . . . AND WARNING

The account of Zacchaeus in Luke 19:1-10 is a wonderful story of transformation. Jesus goes to Jericho where the chief tax collector, a wealthy man named Zacchaeus, who also is short, climbs a sycamore tree in order to see Jesus. When Jesus sees Zacchaeus, he declares, "Zacchaeus, hurry and come down; for I must stay at your house today." Luke tells us that Zacchaeus was "happy to welcome him." The encounter between Jesus and Zacchaeus is extraordinary because Jesus is embracing a man who profits from the Roman occupation of Israel. Zacchaeus made his money from the taxation of his own people. Yet this man, the chief of the tax collectors, is open to being profoundly touched by Jesus. He wants to experience Jesus. Often the retelling of the story ends with Jesus' announcement that he will dine with Zacchaeus, but the story continues.

People were grumbling that Jesus went to be the guest of such a sinner. When Zacchaeus hears this, it pierces his heart and he responds to the transformative presence of Jesus by saying, "Look, half of my possessions, Lord, I will give to the poor; and if I have defrauded anyone of anything, I will pay back four times as much." This is a lavish response by Zacchaeus because he probably defrauded the majority of the people from whom he collected taxes! To pay back four times is extravagant. In delight Jesus declares, "Today salvation has come to this house." Zacchaeus who was lost to salvation is now found. Zacchaeus who had emptiness in his life is now full. Zacchaeus who was wealthy at the expense of other people is now generous toward God and others.

Zacchaeus and I do not seem to share much in common. He was a Jewish male, a tax collector in the first century. I am a woman who grew up in Oklahoma City in the twentieth century. Yet I identify with Zacchaeus in special ways because he and I share similar conversion experiences.

I was born with a silver spoon in my mouth and have never known economic poverty. As a baby boomer I have experienced what it is like to get overextended on credit! But I have never been economically poor without options or help. I struggle to be a good steward of my money. Part of my problem is that money has always been a means to an end for me, so the more I made, the more I adjusted my lifestyle to consume the money. By the age of thirty-nine my life had a great emptiness. On the surface I possessed most of the things that the world tells you one needs to be a success in life—college degree, good job, home, cars, boat, friends, social life, and vacations. But my life lacked a deep sense of fulfillment and accomplishment. I was adrift and needed a savior. By the grace of God, I finally surrendered to Jesus Christ.

I had been a Christian all my life, but since my teen years my participation in church had been nominal. I spent sixteen months of intense searching for God before I encountered the power of self-surrender. Once I was willing to let God be in control, my life dramatically changed. Part of that change involved accepting an invitation to leave my management position at Southwestern Bell Telephone Company and begin seminary studies. This move took me from a comfortable $55,000-a-year salary and great benefits to a student pastorate of $10,800 with no benefits. The transition was a bit of a shock! I was raised to reciprocate gifts and to give to those who are in need. Now I suddenly found myself on the needy list! Through a dozen different ways over the past fourteen years, I have felt the Lord leading me to grapple with economic simplicity.

There are a number of similarities between Zacchaeus's experience and my own. Both of us had to go out of the way to experience the salvation of Christ. Zacchaeus went out on a sycamore limb; I had to search intently for sixteen months for the narrow road. My seeking took me through Bible studies, churches, prayers, ministries, and people. The truth that Zacchaeus and I both found is that when we climb up in a tree and out on a limb to meet Jesus, he will be there for us. Once we encounter the living Christ, two things will happen: We will freely share what we have with others and we will gain a new sense of integrity in our lives. We realize that we too are responsible for becoming who we want to be.

As I work on this manuscript I wonder, By what authority do I address the issue of faithful Christian living in daily economic choices? I must confess that my authority does not come from having achieved economic simplicity in my life. Rather my authority comes from my calling and resultant efforts to learn to be economically faithful in the midst of abundance. The standard that I use in judging my richness is the global standard; I take into account how people live throughout the world. And what I find is that I am a Christian and I am rich!

My faith tells me that being a Christian must affect *who I am* and *how I behave* with my wealth. If my faith is the guide for the path I walk, then Christ has first claim upon my heart and my life. Christ has something to say about the way I live my daily life, from how I treat others to how I spend my money. Faithful stewardship is an issue of integrity and a concern of faith. Jesus does have plenty to say; we just have to discover what it is.

Like Zacchaeus I believe that if we are open to being profoundly touched by the living Christ, we too can grow in our own unique way more fully into the image of the whole, complete human being that God intends for each of us to be. I am convinced that we can each embrace a faithful way of living within our own circumstances.

WARNING: This study is not for the faint of heart! It involves serious reflection and thought. It presents some new and challenging information and stretches your awareness of yourself and the world around you. It certainly is not necessary for you to understand or agree with everything in this workbook. Take what helps you and begin there. Seek only to encounter the Spirit and be led on a path to more faithful and joyful living.

Spiritual formation is the process of being molded into the likeness of Jesus Christ for the sake of those around us. To become conformed to the likeness of Christ involves the three interactive stages of being informed, being formed, and being transformed. The *information* part of the process involves our actively working to gather information about God, about ourselves, and about our commitments. The *formation* stage involves both our doing work and our being worked on by God, while *transformation* is God's work in us.

This workbook consists of an introduction, six weeks of study lessons, and a resources list. The overall structure of the book is to aid the flow of information, formation, and transformation. The first two weeks of information gathering are subtitled *Climbing the Sycamore Tree.* The primary emphases are opening our eyes to the realities of our world and increasing our awareness of key biblical principles. These are the two hardest weeks in the book because there is so much to think about. Remember, take what is helpful and leave what is not helpful.

The second section of two weeks of formation is subtitled *Finding the Zacchaeus in You.* I hope our awareness will continue to grow as we begin to see ourselves better and to see not only with our eyes but with our heart and soul and spirit as well. The final section, *Coming Down the Sycamore Tree,* deals with transformation. Inspired by what we are learning, we will be open to transformation that reflects more clearly the daily living of the faith we confess.

The ideal plan is to do this study in a group, but you can do it on your own too. Each week consists of five self-paced daily sections and one group session. This arrangement uses a Sabbath principle of giving you one or two days off each week. If you are not in a group, please read the group sessions and engage yourself with the questions and activities. If you are doing this study on your own, you may want to take twelve weeks to process it rather than six weeks. Please tailor this study to what works best for you. The daily lessons consist of reading and reflection, and some include activities.

I encourage you to use a journal throughout this study. Keeping a journal helps you to "think through things," getting you in touch with and recording your thoughts and feelings. Looking back over a journal as you journey also is helpful. When I am in a growth period, I find a journal an excellent place for me to continue to reflect upon certain ideas or questions over a period of time. The journal helps me see the progressive development of my thoughts.

And now, let us turn to Week One and begin to consider *Climbing the Sycamore Tree.*

PART ONE

—INFORMATION—
CLIMBING THE
SYCAMORE TREE

Your word is a lamp to my feet
and a light to my path.

—*Psalm 119:105*

WEEK ONE

READ THE FOLLOWING SCRIPTURE
PASSAGE EACH DAY THIS WEEK.

Again Jesus spoke to them, saying, "I am the light of the world. Whoever follows me will never walk in darkness but will have the light of life."

—John 8:12

DAY ONE

CULTURAL CHRISTIANITY

Scripture: Not everyone who says to me, "Lord, Lord," will enter the kingdom of heaven, but only the one who does the will of my Father in heaven.

—Matthew 7:21

Most of us are "cultural Christians." We do not behave economically with any clear understanding of God's biblical instructions to us as followers of Jesus Christ. Rather our lifestyles are shaped and conditioned by our culture, and if the truth be known, most of us worship first the god of mammon, the god of wealth and possessions. It is a blessing for us to be rich; what is wrong is to spend our money as though our faith has no impact on our stewardship.

Two scriptures help inform my economic faith lifestyle, and I believe the overall witness of the Bible supports their importance as a guide for us all. The first is Luke 12:48: "From everyone to whom much has been given, much will be required; and from the one to whom much has been entrusted, even more will be demanded." By the world's standards you and I are wealthy people. We have been entrusted with much, and consequently much is going to be expected of us. The heart of our stewardship lies in delighting God by balancing what we have with how we spend it. Responsibility comes with blessings.

One of the realities about Zacchaeus's money is that it was blood money. I realize that part of our money is tainted too. In a very real sense it is blood money because it is obtained at the expense of other people. We can easily get mixed up with blood money today and not even realize it. Let me give you an example. As a United Methodist minister I invest in a pension program. I have six investment options for my personal contributions: the Diversified Investment Fund, the basic United Methodist pension fund investment portfolio; Domestic Bond Fund, fixed-income securities such as bonds and mortgages; Domestic Stock Fund or International Stock Fund, equity-type securities such as common stock; Money Market Plus Fund, short-term securities such as certificates of deposit; and Balanced Social Values Plus Fund, which includes all types of special funds invested *only* in companies with a positive approach to social issues, companies that strive to enhance the quality of life. In the last fund, money is invested only in life-affirming companies and corporations, in contrast to the other funds in which money is invested in companies and corporations whose primary goal is making money. Any company that does not meet the life-affirming requirements of the Balanced Social Values Fund probably is not going to care how what they do affects the local people. Their chief concern is to make money; money is more important than people and nature. And so I say that the money I would receive from investments in any of the funds except the Social Values one is tainted with blood.

Our temptation is to ignore this kind of association of our money with less-than-ethical uses and go on investing money as though we have a responsibility only to ourselves. That attitude reflects the belief "I am blessed to be blessed" rather than the Abrahamic conviction that we are blessed to be a blessing (Genesis 12:2-3). Luke 12:48 informs me that while I have been richly blessed, God expects me to be generous to others with those blessings. This understanding is amplified by the second key scripture, 1 Timothy 6:17-19:

> As for those who in the present age are rich, command them not to be haughty, or to set their hopes on the uncertainty of riches, but rather on God who richly provides us with everything for our enjoyment. They are to do good, to be rich in good works, generous, and ready to share, thus storing up for themselves the treasure of a good foundation for the future, so that they may take hold of the life that really is life.

This text abounds with rich ideas such as: we are to set our hope on God and not riches; God provides us with everything for our joy; we are called to be generous with others; and following Jesus reflects the way that really is *life*.

As a citizen of the U.S.A., I know that my country is a wealthy one and that it has grown wealthy in part from the labors of those who enjoy few freedoms and who suffer economically. Even with all our wealth, we do not seem joyful or happy as a nation. Rather many in my country are morally and spiritually bankrupt. Is this bankruptcy the result of not being grounded in gratitude to God and generosity to others? Have we lost touch with our heart and our soul? Could we fail to appreciate what we have? Could we have a gnawing emptiness at the center of our lives?

I fear that most of us are claimed more by our culture than by the faith that we espouse. Even as Christians, we tend to be greedy like everyone else and oftentimes are "known" by our possessions. I have seen fancy sports cars whose license tags read: PRAY4IT and ASK GOD. Now that sort of faith statement may be fine until a person drives by and says, "Many of us prayed that my sick child would get well but she died. Is God more interested in providing a car than sustaining life in a child?" As responsible Christians, we must seek to understand both God's relationship with humanity and God's position toward wealth and poverty. A significant part of this workbook seeks these understandings.

The link between the faith we profess and the lifestyle we live is crucial. Today the whole world may depend upon a reversal in economic trends from self-centeredness to faithful stewardship. As Christians, as living witnesses in a secular world, no longer can we believe one thing and act a different way. The faith that truly guides us is reflected in our lifestyles. More often than not, that faith is secular or idolatrous. No longer can I speak of faith apart from the reality of how I live. Faith must inform my thoughts, actions, and behaviors. For all of us, faith must be the central core of our being. We must live our faith in all of our life and not limit our discipleship to particular times or areas.

Reflection: *Where in your life does your faith affect your lifestyle? Write your reflection here.*

Prayer: *Loving One, help us to delight you with our stewardship of our life's resources. Amen.*

DAY TWO

THE WORLD AROUND US

Scripture: Do not be conformed to this world, but be transformed by the renewing of your minds, so that you may discern what is the will of God—what is good and acceptable and perfect.

—Romans 12:2

We are living in a quickly changing world. Think about some of the momentous global changes in the last fifteen years of the twentieth century. In the political arena we have witnessed the collapse of the Soviet Union; the end of the Cold War; the reunification of Germany; the election of democratic governments in some Eastern European states; the end of apartheid in South Africa; the rise of an Armenian nation; the brutal and devastating ethnic wars in Bosnia, Rwanda, the Democratic Republic of the Congo, and Kosovo; as well as the present-day efforts for peace talks between Israel and the PLO and Protestants and Catholics in Northern Ireland. In the economic arena we have witnessed the emerging world market, the rise of giant multinational conglomerate corporations, and the explosion of communication via the internet. Isn't it astounding? It's enough to make your head spin!

Having been born in 1948 I was under the impression that I had lived through the ages of technology and communication. But I have come to realize that the changes taking place this very moment are far broader than technological changes. They are core human changes—changes in the cultural, moral, and spiritual fiber of who we are. It is an exciting and a frightening time to be alive! I think people "sense" this time of earth-shaking change. Many Christians speak to me about our being in the end times, and no doubt we are closer to it today than yesterday. They are react-ing to—and trying to interpret—the massive change taking place in every area of our lives.

A 1995 book by Howard Snyder projects eight global trends over the next thirty-five years: the coming of an instant-access culture, global economy, new roles for women, the environmental revolution, new scientific understandings of matter, the computer culture, the internal decline of Western society, and the power shifts in global politics. Appropriately titled *EarthCurrents: The Struggle for the World's Soul,* Snyder's book states that we are living in a time of global revolution. Likening our time to a hinge of history, Snyder reports that most cultural analysts see epoch change, unparalleled in history, happening now.[1]

Think for a minute about the United States. It has gone from being a Christian nation to being an ethnically and religiously diverse country. Our new secularism car-ries more power than any religious group and seems to espouse an amoral or immoral view of life. There is no longer a commonly understood foundation for ethical deci-sion making. The primary problem in the younger generations is an absence of con-science, while in the older generations it is an erosion of conscience. Money rules as the greatest source of power. In the arena of media and entertainment, the world is viewed through the lenses of sex and violence. Television talk shows resemble freak shows at a fair where the bizarre is touted as normal.

On emotional levels we have so overidentified with the personal lives and plights of criminals that we lose sight of the victims and the sense of responsibility all people have for their actions. In a satirical editorial by Richard Peck, Adam, Eve, and God are in a mock trial regarding the events of Genesis 3. Adam and Eve are found inno-cent while God is found guilty for the sin.[2] After all, didn't God create the snake and the tree of knowledge? By denying Adam and Eve the ability to eat the fruit, didn't God deny them the ability to know right from wrong? A question of obedience? Never. Entrapment? Of course.

In addition to these many and varied changes, we are forgetting how to live together in community. Let me relate a change among people in my own home state of Oklahoma. Since the terrorist bombing of the Murrah Federal Building on April 19, 1995 at 9:02 A.M. none of us has been the same. Things that happen "elsewhere" have happened here. Yes, good has triumphed over evil, but what we are coming to realize is the world, Oklahoma, our own neighbors, are no longer who or what we thought they were. People are different than we are, and different is threatening, life-threatening. We don't all play by the same rules. The Ten Commandments hardly matter anymore.

At a time when we desperately need to move away from fear of difference and all the "isms," such as sexism, racism, and ageism, we are having experiences that tell us we cannot trust others. As Christians we have not been given a spirit of cowardice but of power, love, and self-discipline (2 Timothy 1:7). We must not let the fears abounding in the world create cowardice in us, cowardice that directs our lives and behavior. As Christians we are not devoid of an ethical foundation; we just tend to be ignorant of it. We have a "way" in a wayward world. We have a Guide and a Companion. We have the power to embrace more fully a true Christian way of life. We have the opportunity to bring a vital living faith to bear in our world.

Reflection: *List twenty words to describe your world.*

What is your foundation for the ethical and moral decisions you make in your life? Write your reflection here.

Prayer: *We live in a fast-paced, constantly changing world. Oh God, be to us a rock, an anchor. Show us your path, your way. Amen.*

OUR ADDICTIVE SOCIETY

Scripture: We must no longer be children, tossed to and fro and blown about by every wind of doctrine, by people's trickery, by their craftiness in deceitful scheming. But speaking the truth in love, we must grow up in every way into him who is the head, into Christ.

—*Ephesians 4:14-15*

My Mother used to say that I had a hole in my pocket where money was concerned! A significant amount of my allowance went to purchasing my favorite chocolate when I was a child—M&Ms. Later I experienced addiction to cigarettes. So when I saw Anne Wilson Schaef's book *When Society Becomes an Addict,* I couldn't resist it (no pun intended!). I'm glad I didn't. Her excellent book diagnoses some of the functional problems in the society of the United States of America today. I believe it can speak to other Western societies too.

In her groundbreaking work, Schaef calls the society in which we live an "addictive system." By this Schaef means that our society demonstrates the same characteristics and processes as an individual alcoholic or addict. To say this is not to condemn society but to diagnose its illness; it is to say our society has a disease, and the name of it is *addiction.* Let's look more closely at what it means to call our society addictive.

> An addiction is any process over which we are powerless. It takes control of
> us, causing us to do and think things that are inconsistent with our personal
> values and leading us to become progressively more compulsive and obses-

sive. . . . An addiction keeps us unaware of what is going on inside us. . . . As we lose contact with ourselves, we also lose contact with other people and the world around us. An addiction dulls and distorts our sensory input. . . . An addiction absolves us from having to take responsibility for our lives.[3]

We need to take four healing steps to be free of our disease. We must: 1) *understand* the disease, 2) *notice* our behavior, 3) *name* our behavior for what it is, and 4) *act* to change it. These steps are difficult to take. They all require action on our part and are pieces of a process that unfolds over years, but the rewards are worth the costs.

To help us understand our cultural disease better, Schaef identifies nineteen characteristics and seven processes involved in an addictive system. We will look briefly at five of the characteristics. Those are: the illusion of control, dishonesty, abnormal thinking processes, ethical deterioration, and fear.

The illusion of control and manipulative behavior are the foundations of addictive relationships. None of us can control much of anything, yet we often think we can or ought to be able to control situations. For example, we may wear the "right" clothes, drive the "right" car, say and do the "right" things in order to make someone love us. But love is always a gift freely given. We don't have the power to create love for us in someone else. Trying to control everything in our lives produces crisis, depression, and stress. According to Schaef, the illusion of control is the source of almost all stress.[4]

Dishonesty is the norm within the addictive system. One of the main results of an addiction is becoming detached from thoughts and feelings. Three levels of lying are involved: lying to myself, lying to the people around me, and lying to the world.

Abnormal thinking processes characterize addictive thinking and depend mainly on the linear, rational, and logical thinking processes of the left brain. Assumptions perpetuate the "stinkin' thinkin.'" For example, we may make assumptions about ethnic groups or the neighbors next door. We don't really want to check the facts because we are afraid of what we may find. If reality does not support our way of thinking, then we distort reality to make it fit our assumptions. We do this to justify and support our addictions. Racism is a good example of "stinkin' thinkin.'"

Ethical deterioration is another way to express spiritual bankruptcy. Addiction causes us to lose touch with our sense of ethics. We will steal, lie, deceive, and manipulate whenever these actions aid our addiction, to achieve our end. Fear then makes us dependent upon our addictions in order to exist day by day. We use food, drugs, TV, alcohol, and even religion to numb us to our fears and to reality. In a society that fosters uncertainty and violence, that encourages self-centeredness and "stinkin' thinkin,'" we fear for our very survival.

What is missing in the addictive system is the input of our experience, emotions, intuition, and reality. We have lost the complexities and the wholeness of the interrelatedness of our bodies, souls, and spirits, as well as the intricate interrelationships of all creation. A large part of our problem is our dualistic view of reality. By *dualistic* I mean always seeing things as contrasting pairs or opposites. Dualism is at the very core of our worldview and of the addictive system for two basic reasons, according to Schaef: first, dualism breaks down a very complex universe, giving us the illusion of control, and second, dualism keeps us stuck at oversimplified poles.[5]

There is freeing power in noticing and naming problems. Jesus said it this way, "You will know the truth, and the truth will make you free" (John 8:32). If we can name the realities of our lives, the truth can break us free from illusion and denial. Thus empowered, we can recognize the priorities in life that deserve our time, energy, and money. We can be good stewards of our lives and the resources of creation.

For example, we talk in the United States about having a "solid waste disposal problem." States are always trying to ship their garbage to other states. Is the real problem solid waste? Or is the real problem the consumer-oriented, throwaway society in which we live? If we want to address the solid-waste issue, shouldn't we address trash reduction by recycling and reducing our use of disposable items?

To be free of our addictive, materialistic society necessitates properly and honestly naming reality. We must strip away denial and dishonesty to find and embrace the truth. When we speak of profit, for instance, we need to understand who profits and at what cost to others. There are always costs—a social cost, a cost to the earth, as well as financial costs, but only the financial costs appear in bookkeeping.

We can break the powers of deception and illusion only by looking at the whole picture and acknowledging reality. For instance, at this very moment I can go out and buy a gallon of gasoline for *less* than a gallon of milk. Yet gasoline is a nonrenewable item. When it is gone, it is gone. Milk is a renewable resource; as long as there are cows there will be milk. It would seem the gallon of gasoline would be more valuable than the milk.

This is a lot of information to take in and think about. If one idea has caught your attention, go with it. That idea is your starting place. The purpose of this study is to help each of us take some small steps in spiritual growth and faithfulness with our resources.

We cannot be blind to reality and truth and be spiritually wise. To grow we have to know, but we do not have to be perfect! As Christians seeking Jesus, we will be led to find truths that not only free us but that help us to help others. With God all things are possible!

The addictive system and its participants are not in touch with reality; something artificial, something counterfeit, has taken the primary spot in the addict's heart. We will find as Christians that we can cut through the addictive process by doing what Jesus prescribed: seeking first the kingdom of God and God's righteousness. Then we will lack for nothing (Matthew 6:33).

Reflection: *As you look at your own personal life, can you identify some of the inconsistencies between your thoughts and actions? Name the different ways in which you have been influenced by your culture's addictive system. Write your reflection here.*

Prayer: *O Jesus, give us godly wisdom to look honestly at ourselves in the light of your truth. Help us to see ourselves through your eyes and to remember your steadfast love for us. Amen.*

DAY FOUR

ECONOMICS AS IDOLATRY

Scripture: *No one can serve two masters; for a slave will either hate the one and love the other, or be devoted to the one and despise the other. You cannot serve God and wealth.*

—*Matthew 6:24*

Richard Foster describes our society in the following words:

> Contemporary culture is plagued by the passion to possess. The unreasoned boast abounds that the good life is found in accumulation, that "more is better." Indeed, we often accept this notion without question, with the result that the lust for affluence in contemporary society has become psychotic: it has completely lost touch with reality.[6]

His diagnosis is shocking and biting—"psychotic," "out of touch with reality." Yet can any Christian who steps back and looks at our culture disagree with Foster? I have been thinking about the issue of the gospel in culture. What reflects authentic Christian response to the gospel? We in the West tend to look at Christianity in Asian and African cultures very critically and cautiously, afraid some pagan cultural expression may persist. When it comes to the core issue of God and mammon, how in the world can Westerners say that we embrace an authentic response to the gospel? Indeed we walk dangerously close to the behavior condemned by the prophets of Israel, behavior that led to Israel's destruction and captivity.

Jesus' sermons make clear the reality that we cannot serve both God and mammon (mammon being wealth that includes both money and possessions). But it seems to me that we certainly try to serve both. The Lord does not sit alone upon the throne of our heart. In fact God can hardly get on our throne for all the stuff that is there!

The Ten Commandments tell us not only that we must deal with who or what will be our gods but that God demands the primary position in our lives. All we have belongs to God, and we are called to accountable stewardship and spirituality. For instance, if I make $28,000 a year, it is not my money to do with as I might please. It is God's provision to me and through me, and I must seek God's guidance and wisdom in spending it.

Some of our cultural stinkin' thinkin' affects our behavior. The scarcity and the zero-sum models are destructive assumptions that direct much of our activity. The scarcity model is based on the assumption that there is not enough of anything to go around; therefore, we had better get as much as we can while we can. This thinking of course leads to hoarding money, material goods, love, prestige, and the list goes on. The false or dishonest solution is: More is always better!

The zero-sum model postulates that if someone else gets something, it will not be there when I need it. According to this view, everything is available in limited, finite quantities. Hence, we not only want more, we want what others have!

Our national addiction to consumption places economics at the heart of our daily lives. E. F. Schumacher shows the insanity of our economic system in his book *Small is Beautiful*. Under the false assumption that everything has a price, civilization assigns its highest value to money.[7] My question is, If money has the highest value, where do love, truth, integrity, or happiness fit in? How important are people? land? God?

Treating money as the highest value reflects a confusion between ends and means to ends. In our global economy goods are not valued according to identification as primary goods (natural products won from nature) or secondary goods (manufactured products requiring primary products for production). The sole criterion of "value" in a product is its potential for profitable distribution.

Our present-day economic system lacks an ethical foundation. The first commandment of the religion of economics is to behave economically. In other words, make the most profit possible regardless of the true cost of the product or the human and environmental cost for production or consumption. My example about the present-day cost for one gallon of gasoline versus one gallon of milk reflects a result of this rationale.

Again it seems that our economics are based on the illusions of control and power, manifested in the value attached to profit making rather than to the intrinsic nature of things, ethics, accountability, or responsibility. We are operating in what John Kavanaugh calls a "commodity form" of economics.[8] In this way of life the most important values are marketability and consumption. People are not ends in themselves but means to the economic market. People are objects of production and consumption and not precious and loved children of the living God.

Activity: Spend some time today with your checkbook. How much is your debt in relation to your income? How much do you give away? Where do you spend your money—utilities? mortgage? car? travel? shopping? electronics? gadgets? knickknacks? entertainment/eating out? church/charities? gifts/presents?

Prayer: O Lord Jesus, you walked the earth with absolute trust in God's provision. Your life was so utterly different than our own. Come show us how to embrace your values within the culture and time in which we live. Amen.

DAY FIVE

MATTERS OF ECONOMICS

Scripture: *What will it profit them to gain the whole world and for-feit their life?*

—Mark 8:36

God saw everything that he had made, and indeed, it was very good" (Genesis 1:31). As Christians we know that all of God's creation is good and valuable. Our Creator intimately interwove our world for shalom, for harmony and wholeness. Contemporary awareness of ecology has revealed that this fragile interconnectedness is endangered. In fact, life on earth is at risk because of the behavior of individuals and groups. Hence we live in a time when people must understand the local and global impact of personal action. The scenario of interconnectedness offered by Laura Meagher in her book *Teaching Children about Global Awareness* was enlightening to me.

Wendy's brother drives her to soccer practice because she doesn't "feel" like walking. While he's out, he drives around burning up a gallon of gas. Now multiply that gallon by the thousands of other unnecessary car trips each day. (According to Meagher, by the time you read this sentence more than forty thousand gallons of gas will be burned by U.S. drivers!) Now give some Middle Eastern petroleum producers the profits from those gasoline sales. In the Middle East, owning an ivory-hilt dagger is a sign of prosperity. Some of these producers will purchase such daggers, leading to an increased demand for ivory. This increased demand leads to the killing of elephants for their ivory in several African countries. (According to Meagher the elephant population was halved between 1979 and 1989.) An elephant eats about three hundred pounds of vegetation a day. The process of the elephants' feeding creates open spaces and water holes for other animals. Without the elephants' activity, the environment becomes detrimental to other forms of life. The question is, whose fault is the slaughter of elephants in Africa? Are the Wendys of the world to blame?[9]

Meagher's question is one we might like to ignore, but in accountable economics, we must face it and struggle for responsible answers and alternatives. Every one of us is responsible for the earth's resources. Most of us are familiar with the three Rs—reduce, reuse, and recycle. As Christians we must add a fourth R—redistribute. We should be active in the redistribution of materials and wealth to help those in need. We will look more at redistribution when we turn to the Bible for an understanding of God's position on wealth and poverty.

Have you ever wondered how it was that we became the way we are—an addictive, materialistic society? I was curious and found a book by Laurence Shames, *The Hunger for More,* which provided some insights. Shames says the unparalleled affluence of America in the 1950s became the reference point of normalcy, the standard.[10] Shames essentially attributes America's abnormal affluence to our lack of physical devastation and resultant rebuilding after World War II. The U.S. was untouched by bombs, political upheavals, or the diluted dollar (save Hawaii, which was then not a state). We had an enormous economic head start compared to the rest of the "developed world." In fact, America stood alone economically, and this status was not normal.

During the post–World War II years, the U.S. experienced the phenomenon called the baby boom. Our population increased by almost 50 percent between 1946 and 1964. Coupled with the population explosion was an unprecedented explosion of technological creativity. In 1953 we contained 7 percent of the world's population, yet we produced 67 percent of its manufactured products, owned 75 percent of its appliances and cars, and purchased 33 percent of the world's goods and services! General Motors's operating budget was greater than Poland's. It is amazing that a whole country could be run on a budget smaller than that of a single major corporation. Americans spent more on entertainment than it cost to run the country of

Switzerland. None of these facts reflected normal world balances of the past when the developed nations had been much closer in measures of production and expenditures. "Was it normal that a higher proportion of dwellings in the city of Chicago should be equipped with television sets than with bathtubs, or that the average American should consume three and a half times as much food as the average foreigner, or that his income should be fifteen times as great . . . ?" asks Laurence Shames in *The Hunger for More.*[11] No, none of these facts was normal. Yet these statistics set the stage for what we now consider to be normal.

We have become a consumer-based society with insatiable appetites. Our first concern is to get what we want without considering the cost, if any, to other people, the environment, or future generations. We are very much a "me first" society. How do we get free from the addictions to consumption and superficiality? How do we get free from the illusion of control and the rampant self-centeredness that characterize us? The answer is, not without a lot of hard work, a lot of prayer, and a lot of God's grace. You have made a start in this direction by engaging in this study. If you did the activity yesterday, you have begun to wrestle with your own personal economics.

As the new year dawned in 1992, I felt certain God was calling me to make a vow of simplicity in my daily economic life. For that year I was to spend my money on maintenance, repairs, and consumables only. In other words, I would not buy any clothes, gadgets, knickknacks, vacation mementos, and so forth. In January when I was between semesters in seminary, I went on a wonderful silent retreat to Lebh Shomea Retreat Center, located about sixty miles south of Corpus Christi, Texas. While I was there, several dreams seemed to confirm this simplicity vow, as well as point to the importance of my taking this vow seriously. I left feeling graced to return to the world and embrace my vow.

Well, my first serious temptation took place in Corpus Christi at the airport on my return home! I am a water person and love shells. One of the stores had a perfectly formed and beautiful purple urchin shell. It was a mere seventy-five cents, and I could not buy it because of my vow. Seventy-five cents, for heaven's sake; a soda cost me more! But I knew the battle lines were drawn, and my retreat experience had empowered me with the grace to resist and go on.

That year was a wonderful experience in my life. The Lord had called me, and the Lord had empowered me to succeed. My birthday gifts to people were consumable foods and drinks they liked. My Christmas gifts were donations to different charities in their names. I have not had another year like it, but I hope God will lead me again to such a vow.

Activity: Look at the results of your checkbook analysis from yesterday. How much of the money you spend is for essentials? for nonessentials? (You may need to give some thought to what is "essential" and "nonessential." I do consider both spiritual retreats and vacations as essentials for most busy people.) Look at your nonessentials. How much is frivolous? Did you buy things you didn't need?

Prayer: Giver of all good gifts, help us to trust your love for us! Help us to realize the materialistic insanity that sometimes possesses us. Help us to choose less stuff and more of you, the Giver. Amen.

ECONOMIC STRUGGLES

Note: These sessions are first and foremost for the particular group that is meeting, so feel free to adapt these sessions to meet your specific needs. Based on the size of the group, you may wish to form smaller groups for different activities. If a particular group size is desirable for a particular exercise, it will be so noted.

Opening Prayer

Creating God, we gather today as a group, a small community of your children. We come seeking to understand your word and your call for us to be molded into the likeness of Christ for the world. You are the God of life and love. May your Spirit be present among us to nurture our growth in knowledge and information. Amen.

Group Interaction Exercise (Allow twenty minutes.)

Go around the group and introduce yourselves by providing your name and sharing three statements about yourself, two of which are true and one of which is false. The group will guess which statement is false.

Activity (Allow fifteen minutes.)

Divide into groups of three or four to brainstorm and discuss the following topics. Have someone in each group take notes or summarize on newsprint.

1. Brainstorm and create a pool of words that describes the society in which we live.
2. What meaning or implications do these words project about our understanding of the world?

Reconvene the large group and let representatives from each small group share highlights from the discussions, perhaps three words and what each suggests about our understanding of the world.

Discussion (Allow twenty minutes.)
Again in small groups discuss the following questions.

1. How does society's lust for affluence affect you? Take some time to let each person explain his or her answer.
2. Does evaluating your own economic behavior (as in this week's activities) give you a better perspective on society's influence? If yes, in what way? If no, what might make the connection between society's expectations and your behavior concrete for you?
3. If a gallon of gasoline costs $1.50, how much should a gallon of milk cost? Why? What are your rationalizations?

When the larger group reconvenes, share each group's cost for a gallon of milk along with reasons for that price.

Engaging Scripture (Allow fifteen minutes.)
Read the parable of the laborers in the vineyard in Matthew 20:1-16. Let members of the group turn to their neighbor and discuss the following:

- What do you think was unfair about the landlord's behavior?
- What do you think was fair about the landlord's behavior?
- This is one of Jesus' "kingdom-of-heaven-is-like" parables. What does that mean to you?

In the large group share the most important insights from this scripture study with one another.

Closing

As a closing prayer, share this prayer of confession.

Lord, we confess our day-to-day failure to be truly human.
Lord, we confess to you.

Lord, we confess that we often fail to love with all we have and are, often because we do not fully understand what loving means, often because we are afraid of risking ourselves.
Lord, we confess to you.

Lord, we cut ourselves off from one another and we erect barriers of division.
Lord, we confess to you.

Lord, we confess that by silence and ill-considered word
we have built up walls of prejudice.

Lord, we confess that by selfishness and lack of sympathy
we have stifled generosity and left little time for others.

Holy Spirit, speak to us. Help us listen to your word of forgiveness, for we are very deaf. Come, fill this moment and free us from sin.[12]

Let us remember and take comfort in the knowledge that when we are faithful to confess our sins, God is faithful to forgive our sins! Alleluia! Amen!

WEEK TWO

READ THE FOLLOWING SCRIPTURE
PASSAGE EACH DAY THIS WEEK.

Just then a lawyer stood up to test Jesus. "Teacher," he said, "what must I do to inherit eternal life?" He answered, "You shall love the Lord your God with all your heart, and with all your soul, and with all your strength, and with all your mind; and your neighbor as yourself." And he said to him, "You have given the right answer; do this, and you will live."

—Luke 10:25-28

DAY ONE

IN THE IMAGE OF GOD

Scripture: *So God created humankind in his image, in the image of God he created them; male and female he created them.*

—Genesis 1:27

These words from Genesis 1:27 have given humans a privileged position in creation. We alone are said to be made in the image of God. It sounds simple, but what does it mean? Are we like God in our appearance? our mental capabilities? Take time now to reflect on being made in God's image in three ways:

- as social and relational creatures,
- as persons with free will, and
- as people who make moral choices.

These may be different ways of reflecting on God's image in us than you have thought about before. I offer them as food for thought.

Perhaps one of the most amazing statements in the account of humans' creation is God's self-reference as "us." God says, "Let us make humankind in our image, according to our likeness" (Genesis 1:26). Is God not one God? How then can God be "us"? Like many people, I believe there is only one God and that this statement at creation reflects the essential unity and relatedness of the Trinity. At creation the Spirit of God sweeps over the waters and formless void of the earth. Then God's creating happens through the spoken Word: "Then God *said,* . . ." (1:3). The gospel writer John identifies Jesus as the Word made flesh. So in the opening words of scripture we have God the Creator, the Spirit, and the Word. By referring to God's self as "us," God reveals a social and relational nature.

While the first creation story gives us a magnificent account of an awesome God of power and order, the second account in Genesis 2 reveals an intimate God. The second story changes the order of creation: God forms the first human out of the dust of the earth, then breathes the breath of life into the human (Genesis 2:7). God places the person in the Garden of Eden and creates all the animals as helpers and partners. Both accounts show us, in different ways, the radical interconnectedness of all creation. We are not creatures independent of the moon and stars, the seasons of the year, or the birds of the air. God created us all to live together in shalom—that rich Hebrew word that means peace, wholeness, harmony, and completeness. Our relationships are going to be important places for us in reflecting God's image.

The creation accounts reveal another characteristic of God—free will. Nothing forces God to create. Creation is a radical and risky free choice on God's part. Our Creator has gifted each of us with the freedom of choice. What if we, those made in this holy image, reject God? The choice is ours. What if we refuse to share with one another and are greedy and violent toward one another? God has given us the choice.

After placing the first human in the Garden of Eden, God commands, "You may freely eat of every tree of the garden; but of the tree of the knowledge of good and evil you shall not eat, for in the day that you eat of it you shall die" (Genesis 2:16). God establishes boundaries on our freedom. Some things are off limits. Today we continue to struggle with our boundaries in relationships with people and with the earth.

In a similar sense, the Creator has chosen to set boundaries for God's self too. God cannot violate who God is. God's integrity is perfect. For instance, God loves us, and therefore God cannot hate us. God can allow us to do evil, but God cannot hate us if we do. Similarly, God will not force any of us to do something; nor will God restrain us from doing what we have made up our mind to do. The Creator will not violate God's own gift of free will to us. Does this mean that our Maker is not active in our choices? No. I think if we look at our circumstances we will see where God has been seeking to get our attention. God will try to warn our conscience of bad choices as well as woo us to good choices.

Like our Creator, we possess both freedom and limitations. The big difference is that God is in charge of the boundaries. Our freedom is limited by boundaries; God's freedom is limitless, yet God imposes limitations on God's self as a matter of integrity.

A third way in which we are made in God's image is in our ability to discern good from evil. Life calls upon us to make moral choices. God is a God of good and has created a world with both good and evil, right and wrong. As God distinguishes between right and wrong intentions and actions, so God has equipped us with both the ability and the responsibility to make good moral choices. Choosing between obviously good and bad options isn't hard; picking the lesser of two evils or the better of two good choices can be quite difficult.

As creatures made in the image of God we are called to uphold the principles and standards of God. As Christians, we will understand these most clearly in terms of the moral values that energized the life of Jesus Christ.

Reflection: Which way of imagining God most speaks to you?

- *God as a social and relational being*
- *God as a possessor of free will*
- *God as a maker of moral choices*

How have you always understood being "made in the image of God"? What would you add to the ways discussed above? Write your reflection here.

Prayer: *O God who made us in your image, empower us to display that image in wise and loving ways. Amen.*

DAY TWO

IN THE LIKENESS OF CHRIST

Scripture: Let the same mind be in you that was in Christ Jesus.

—Philippians 2:5

A couple of years ago I read a story that has taken on great metaphorical significance for me. The setting is Christmas Eve in Chicago in the 1920s, before the stock market crash. Two businessmen are rushing to catch the 6:00 P.M. commuter train for home. On the train platform a young handicapped boy is selling papers and other goods he can pick up and resell for a bargain at a small stand. The first man emerges on the platform. He runs into the boy, knocking him and his stand over. Hurling a few choice curse words at the boy, the man continues on to catch his train. A few seconds later the second man emerges on the platform. He sees the boy and his stand knocked down. He immediately helps the boy up and tries to gather up some of his goods. The man reaches in his billfold and pulls out a five-dollar bill. He gives it to the boy, saying he hopes it will help cover part of the boy's losses. Wishing the boy a "Merry Christmas," he turns to catch his train. The boy yells after him, "Say, Mister, are you Jesus Christ?" Red-faced and embarrassed, the man answers, "No, but I try to be like him."

Both men are made in the image of God, but only one man is living in the likeness of Jesus Christ. It is not enough as a Christian to claim being made in our Creator's image; we are called to be conformed to the likeness of Christ. This is the hard part of the gospel where Jesus says we have to die in order to live, to pick up our cross and follow him, to seek first the kingdom of God and all else will be given to us. If we are to be in the likeness of Jesus Christ, we need to reflect upon the values that energized his life. We will look at three values:

- righteousness
- compassion
- justice

Jesus' relationship with his Father is one that we can only imagine from glimpsing our own closest moments with God. That Jesus was *righteous,* in right standing with God, is beyond any shadow of question or doubt. In John 5:30 Jesus says, "I can do nothing on my own. As I hear, I judge; and my judgment is just, because I seek to do not my own will but the will of him who sent me." Repeatedly Jesus went apart to spend intense periods of time in the presence of his Father. These periods helped shape and mold Jesus into the righteous image of God.

Mark 6:3 tells us that Jesus was a carpenter. Aside from this we know nothing of his life between the ages of twelve and thirty. But this we do know: as soon as Jesus initiates his mission and ministry by publicly announcing his baptism, the Spirit draws him away to forty days of fasting, prayer, and testing. Obediently Jesus allows himself to be drawn apart. While obedience is not synonymous with righteousness, one cannot be righteous without being faithfully obedient. These periods of abiding in God produce a profound sense of righteousness in Jesus. The same sense of righteousness will be ours if we take the time to open to God in our lives. As we sense God's leading and walk in that way, we will grow righteous too. We will be people of integrity and honesty, abiding in God's spirit.

The adjective that most describes Jesus for me is *compassionate.* Jesus identifies with the marginalized and outcasts, with women and children, with Gentiles and sinners. Over and over we read that Jesus has compassion on crowds and on individuals. He stands with these people and ministers to them. No one is too unclean or too great a sinner for Jesus. He generously embraces and loves all. He offers himself freely to all people. John's Gospel is clearest in fleshing out what it means to love our neighbor as ourselves: it is to love as Jesus loves (13:34). The mark of discipleship is to love as Jesus loves, with compassion and self-giving. Serving as an end-of-life chaplain for Hospice Austin in Austin, Texas, has been a great blessing for me. There I am able to care for a very diverse population of people, as I participate in a secular nonprofit organization that operates out of the love ethic Jesus taught.

Jesus also highly values and embodies justice. *Justice* is not to be understood as fairness in a competitive context but rightness and justness that reflect the values of God. God's ways usually are inverted to human ways. In our world the weak and the poor remain oppressed and the powerful rule. In God's kingdom the rich will be brought low and the poor exalted. For Jesus, as for God, each person is of equal value to other persons. Love is the rule that guides our relationships with family, friends, strangers, and even enemies. God's justice is grounded in love and equality.

Being a responsible citizen of our community is a way to enact justice in our daily life. Vote, speak out on issues, notice problems—especially unfair situations. I recall a poor ethnic area with terrible street drainage in a large town where I lived. When enough other neighborhoods called city officials on this neighborhood's behalf, the city council agreed to do something about the problem. The poor people's streets were repaired because people spoke out on their behalf.

Any of us seeking a life in the likeness of Christ must embrace righteousness born of and nurtured by relationship with God. Our guiding moral principle for living will be justness and rightness as viewed through the eyes of God and not the world's. And the glue, the power that holds all of life together, must be compassionate love. Fortunately we are not expected to be perfect, only faithful!

Reflection: In what ways are you most like Christ? Can you be like Christ without intentionally trying? Write your reflection here.

Prayer: O Loving God, our ways are not your ways. Thanks be for that! Help us to treasure the values that matter most to you. Help us to be more like Jesus in all our relationships. May our discipleship be visible and bring glory to you. Amen.

A COVENANT PEOPLE— MARKED BY LOVE

Scripture: We know love by this, that he laid down his life for us— and we ought to lay down our lives for one another.

—*1 John 3:16*

If we want to be serious about our Christian faith, then we have to take seriously our baptismal covenant with God. The Western world today is plagued by pseudocovenants— commitments that last only as long as they are convenient—whether financial, marriage, or other commitments. Yet the heart of being Christian is rooted in the concept of covenant. We are a covenant people—children and heirs of a covenant-making God. We are ushered into covenant with the Almighty through the water and Spirit of our baptism.

As Christians we inherit all the covenants of our foreparents, but the most binding covenant on us is that made with God through Jesus Christ. There are two primary aspects of our covenant: love and equality. Before we explore those aspects, let me first say a word about *covenant* itself.

God is the initiator of covenant, and we are the recipients and the responders to God. In its most fundamental nature, covenant speaks of who God will be toward us. When Moses demanded to know who was sending him to Egypt, God replied, "I am who I am" (Exodus 3:14) or as can be inferred from Hebrew, "I am who I will be" or "I am who I am becoming." God's name wasn't connected with *doing* but with *being*.

We often think of *covenant* merely as a form of contract—an arrangement of what we will do for one another. But covenant speaks of who we are for one another. For instance, in making wedding vows we commit to a relationship. In a wedding *covenant* we say who we will *be* for each other—for better or worse, for richer or poorer, in sickness and in health, until death do us part. At the same time, we may make a wedding contract that states our children will be raised in the Catholic faith or that in the event of one spouse's death, the deceased's estate items brought into the marriage will revert to his or her first family. Wedding agreements and contracts can be detrimental when they are defined by *doing* rather than *being,* for if you cease to be able to "do," you can be abandoned in divorce. Keep in mind that generally speaking covenants speak of *being* and contracts of *doing* as we reflect on Jesus' covenant of love and equality. Today we will look at the covenant nature of love.

One of the most quoted biblical texts is John 3:16: "For God so loved the world that he gave his only Son, so that everyone who believes in him may not perish but may have eternal life." Speaking to Nicodemus as that passage continues, Jesus goes on to say, "Indeed, God did not send the Son into the world to condemn the world, but in order that the world might be saved through him" (John 3:17). Jesus came because of God's love for us. He came not to condemn us but to reveal who God is and to show us the way to God. Jesus came as a reconciler to join us in right relationship with God in a new and powerful way. Christianity is rooted, grounded, and embodied in God's love for all of us.

No one was so unclean or so sinful that they could repulse Jesus. According to all four gospel accounts, Mary Magdalene, who was cleansed of seven demons, was the first witness to the resurrection. Tradition identifies her as the sinful woman who is forgiven much. In Luke 7:36-50 we read of a woman who brought an alabaster jar of ointment, bathed Jesus' feet with her tears, kisses, and ointment, and then dried his feet with her hair. When Jesus' Pharisee guest reacts to her as a sinner, Jesus tells the story of two debtors whose creditor cancels their debts. One owed five hundred denarii and the other fifty. Jesus asks, Who will love him more? All of us know the answer, the one with the greater debt. In the following passage Luke lists Mary Magdalene as one of the women who travel with Jesus and provide for him and his male disciples out of their own resources (8:1-3).

At the Last Supper Jesus instituted what we call the sacrament of Holy Communion. Matthew tells us that after Jesus took bread and said new words about it, he took a cup and gave thanks. Then Jesus gave the cup to his disciples and said, "Drink from it, all of you; for this is my blood of the covenant, which is poured out for many for the forgiveness of sins" (Matthew 26:27-28). Our covenant was purchased at the cost of Christ's life on the cross. It is sealed by his blood. The covenant in Jesus reveals a God of love and total sacrificial commitment to us. This covenant is empowered through Jesus' resurrection and the gift of the Holy Spirit. At the heart of this love is forgiveness that has the power to reconcile God and us. Christ's covenant is first and foremost a covenant of love. How blessed we are when this reality begins to blossom in our lives!

Reflection: When have you realized God's love for you? What were the circumstances? How did the realization make you feel? Write your reflection here.

Prayer: *Precious Lord, we are not a people who appeared on this earth by happenstance. We are God's children, created in love and for love. Thank you for giving your all for me. May your blood not be spilled in vain. Amen.*

A COVENANT PEOPLE— MARKED BY EQUALITY

Scripture: *There is no longer Jew or Greek, there is no longer slave or free, there is no longer male and female; for all of you are one in Christ Jesus.*

—*Galatians 3:28*

Baptism—our entry into covenant with Jesus Christ—makes us a part of his *universal* covenant. In the global village where we now live, a universal covenant takes on increased significance. We must know how to be Christlike in this global environment. Our starting point is to ground our faith as Christians in our covenant with God *through Jesus Christ*.

I love and treasure the book of Isaiah. But in chapter 43, as in numerous historical events reported in the Old Testament, the favoritism shown to Israel at the expense of other peoples disturbs me. In our love covenant with Jesus Christ there is no room for such favoritism. In Christ "there is no longer Jew or Greek, there is no longer slave or free, there is no longer male and female; for all of you are one in Christ Jesus" (Galatians 3:28).

Along with love, equality among people is a key component of the new covenant in Jesus' blood. To be true to Jesus, the church must embrace equality. In the New Testament Jesus names Peter as the rock upon which he will build his church. When Jesus and his disciples are at Caesarea Philippi, he asks his disciples, "But who do you say that I am?" (Matthew 16:15). Peter responds that Jesus is the Messiah. Jesus in turn responds to Peter, "You are Peter, and on this rock I will build my church and the gates of Hades will not prevail against it" (16:18). The Giver of Life gives Peter an experience to help him understand the radical equality of Christ's love, his encounter with the Gentile Cornelius, which is related in Acts 10, 11, and 15.

Both Cornelius and Peter receive visions from God. Peter's vision illustrates the importance of equality. While at prayer on the roof Peter becomes hungry. He then sees heaven open and a large sheet coming down covered with unclean animals. Peter hears a voice saying, "Get up, Peter; kill and eat" (Acts 10:13). Peter answers, "By no means, Lord; for I have never eaten anything that is profane or unclean" (verse. 14). The voice responds, "What God has made clean, you must not call profane" (verse 15).

As Peter ponders this vision, Cornelius' men arrive seeking Peter. After going to Cornelius' house and hearing his story, Peter exclaims, "I truly understand that God shows no partiality, but in every nation anyone who fears him, and does what is right is acceptable to him" (verses 34-35). Peter is the rock because his testimony to the church at Jerusalem and at the Council of Jerusalem grounds salvation in the free grace of the Lord Jesus revealed through the outpouring of the Holy Spirit. Christ and Christianity are open to all. The covenant of Jesus is for all people. God is doing a new thing in Jesus of Nazareth, and I for one am so glad he is!

The intrinsic moral value of each person is inherent in this understanding of covenant equality. In other words, people are not valued because of their usefulness. People are not means to an end. Each person has an intrinsic worth equal to that of every other person in the sight of God, simply by virtue of possessing the gift of life. As humans we tend to assign worth in conjunction with productivity or other values. From the human perspective, a business executive has more worth or value than a mentally handicapped adult. Not so in God's eyes. The two people are of equal worth to God. Jesus died as much for one as he did for the other. Both people are called to relationship with God through Jesus Christ. Both people are called to discipleship that embraces the values that energized the life of Jesus. Both people are called to be conformed to the image of Christ for the sake of Creation, in the unique ways relevant to their lives.

> **Reflection:** *Do you really believe we are all equal in God's sight? Does knowing that God loves and values others as much as God loves you affect your sense of responsibility for others? Write your reflection here.*

> **Prayer:** *Help us, Lord Jesus, to find joy in the gift of life itself rather than needing to feel superior to others in order to justify ourselves. Help us realize that in Christ we are all sisters and brothers. Amen.*

COVENANT ECONOMICS

Scripture: *Since there will never cease to be some in need on the earth, I therefore command you, "Open your hand to the poor and needy neighbor in your land."*

—Deuteronomy 15:11

We have spent the past four days understanding the foundation of our relationship with God. Today we talk about covenant economics, that is, the economic relationship among covenant members. Let's look at some fundamentals regarding covenant relationship between and among people.

The Ten Commandments are found both in Exodus 20 and in Deuteronomy 5. The first three commandments address our relationship with God. The other seven speak to our relationship with one another within a covenant community formed by God. For example, we are not to steal, murder, commit adultery, or covet because such behaviors divide and separate people. Those behaviors destroy trust and erode a sense of covenant community.

Interestingly the commandments are predicated on what God has done for Israel. In the first commandment God says, "I am the Lord your God, who brought you out of the land of Egypt, out of the house of slavery; you shall have no other gods before me" (Exodus 20:2-3). Later, in chapter 23:9, God commands that Israel "not oppress a resident alien; you know the heart of an alien, for you were aliens in the land of Egypt." It matters not if the biblical text is addressing the twentieth generation of Israelites, the memories of captivity and deliverance are expected to be kept as active memories that hold the power to determine today's behavior toward one another.

Another important concept in the Law is that of sabbatical years. Sabbatical years are grounded in the Sabbath commandment and address two of God's special concerns: human forgetfulness and the need to care for the poor and oppressed. Exodus 23:10-12 contains God's direction to sow and gather for six years and then in the seventh year to allow the land to rest. Its produce shall feed the poor. The same procedure is commanded for vineyards and olive orchards. God knows our hearts well, and it is our nature to believe we possess that which comes into our hands. The commandment to observe the seventh-year Sabbath reminds people that the land belongs to God, and it assures that the poor are cared for.

But the poor do not have to wait seven years to eat. The most famous example of a poor person's gleaning from the field of another is in the story of Ruth. Ruth goes to Boaz's field to glean ears of grain. After meeting Ruth, Boaz goes beyond the call of duty to ensure that his men allow her to glean even among the standing sheaves. He tells the workers to pull out handfuls of grain for her and leave them in the field (Ruth 2:15-16).

Throughout biblical history *need* has been the determining factor in economic relationships among covenant members. The moral holiness code of the Old Testament calls Israel to respect the worth of all people and to care for one another (see Exodus 23 and Leviticus 19 for examples). Covenant economics establishes an economics of equality based on need. Need determines the distribution of resources within the Israelite community: all are to be provided for. The provision of manna in the wilderness is a good example of covenant economics (Exodus 16).

Understanding covenant economics has important consequences. Need is the cornerstone for the distribution of resources. Love for God is to be expressed not only toward God but also toward the neighbor, especially the needy. In the Book of Acts we find an excellent insight into covenant economics in the early Christian community in Jerusalem. Acts 4:45 sums it up well: "They would sell their possessions and goods and distribute the proceeds to all, as they had need." Need determined people's economic behavior. When a need arose that could not be met, someone sold something to provide the funds to meet the need. Covenant relationship is more important than possessions; people are more important than things.

Covenant means all are entitled to be cared for by the community. If people are hungry or needy, somehow the "system" has broken down. The cause of a breakdown could be a social change beyond one's control, such as being widowed or orphaned. But by law (and this is the key point) the responsibility to ensure that all are cared for rests with the wealthy, the privileged, reflecting God's initiative to deliver slaves from their Egyptian captivity.

Perhaps it seems easy to think of covenant economics during the periods of time when the Bible was being written, while to think of practicing it today is foreign and uncomfortable for most of us. Yet believing that God has an inclusive love covenant with all humanity and that God calls us to moral responsibility for the other members of the covenant has radical implications. This belief calls us to consider how we personally can be involved in covenant economics, a system in which the privileged take initiative to redistribute resources to those in need.

> *Reflection: Ponder the invitation to be a part of God's love covenant with all humanity and the consequences. Who is a part of your covenant community? For whom do you experience a sense of Christian responsibility? How do you feel toward people you help with your tax dollars? Do they belong to your covenant community? Write your reflection here.*

How do you honestly feel toward the poor and unfortunate? Check all the statements with which you agree:

1) *They get what they deserve.*
2) *Most people who are poor are poor because of their own behavior.*
3) *In this day and age no one has to be poor.*
4) *Many poor people cannot help being poor. They have little control over their circumstances.*
5) *It is easy to get some kind of job today.*
6) *Most poor people are women and children.*
7) *There should be a welfare system.*
8) *The rich must help assume the cost of necessities for the poor.*
9) *God is especially concerned with the poor.*
10) *I have acquaintances who are "dirt poor."*
11) *I don't know anyone who is "dirt poor."*

Prayer: *Lord, help us to recognize your incredible, steadfast love for each one of us. Forgive our selfishness and help us to respond to your love with joy, gratitude, and generosity. Amen.*

GROUP SESSION

COVENANT ECONOMICS

Opening Prayer

God of grace and glory, God of power and gentleness, we acknowledge ourselves as your creation, your children. You have placed us in a world of competition, yet you call us to be people of justice. You have given us the power of free will, yet you call us to love one another as you love us. You have blessed us materially and economically, yet you call us to share with those less blessed. Help us to welcome your spirit today. Help us to open to your work within and among us. Amen.

Discussion (Allow ten to fifteen minutes.)

Discuss the following questions.

- What feelings do you have in response to this week's readings? Describe immediate reactions and later reflections.
- After reading Luke 10:25-28 each day, have you noticed different aspects of the text? Does the text hold new or different meaning for you now?

Activity (Allow thirty to forty minutes.)

Working in small groups or pairs, first define the community where you live. What are its ethnic makeup, age profile, and economic characteristics? Who are the needy? Who has the resources? Who are the major players?

Jesus reduced all the laws and commandments to one with two components: "to love God with all your heart and soul, mind and strength, and to love your neighbor as yourself." How is this lived out in your geographic community?

Secondly, make a list of different types of community that exist in the world, such as the natural world and the political community. After you develop a list, identify issues or concerns in each area. Can you identify a responsibility for Christians in each area? Share your findings together in the large group.

Closing

As a closing prayer, read Psalm 100 responsively.

Make a joyful noise to the Lord, all the lands.
Serve the Lord with gladness! Come into God's presence with singing!

Know that the Lord, who made us, is God.
We are the Lord's; we are the people of God, the sheep of God's pasture.

Enter God's gates with thanksgiving and God's courts with praise.
Give thanks and bless God's name!

For the Lord is good.
God's steadfast Love endures forever; God's faithfulness to all generations.

PART TWO

—FORMATION—

FINDING THE

ZACCHAEUS IN YOU

I treasure your word in my heart,
so that I may not sin against you.

—*Psalm 119:11*

WEEK THREE

Martha was distracted by her many tasks; so she came to him and asked, "Lord, do you not care that my sister has left me to do all the work by myself? Tell her then to help me." But the Lord answered her, "Martha, Martha, you are worried and distracted by many things; there is need of only one thing. Mary has chosen the better part, which will not be taken away from her."

—Luke 10:40-42

DAY ONE

SIMPLICITY

Scripture: Behold, now is the acceptable time; behold, now is the day of salvation.

—*2 Corinthians 6:2,* RSV

Experience has convinced me that despite our personal desires we grow and mature physically. We will all either grow up and grow old or we will die young. We can do things to keep fit and try to look younger, but regardless of what we do, the biological time clock ticks away. On the other hand, if we want to grow and mature emotionally, spiritually, or relationally, that growth will not just happen. In fact it will happen only if we intentionally seek to grow and mature. So it is with simplicity.

To introduce our discussion on simplicity let us look at the concept in a broad or general sense. Simplicity is not:

- poverty,
- a renunciation of possessions,
- an extreme asceticism based on a division of the world into the spiritual (good) and the material (evil),
- legalism or a set of dos and don'ts.

Simplicity is:

- a spiritual discipline that reorients life,
- a way of life that shuns the artificiality and alienation of contemporary personal and interpersonal life,

- a way of life that challenges affluent consumerism yet allows enjoyment of possessions,
- freedom of the spirit within and of the body without,
- an integrated life lived in harmony with all of creation.

Many people and things compete for our time, energy, and money. Our lives are pulled in many directions. If asked to validate our lives' priorities, most of us would be hard-pressed to reveal lives that support our listed priorities. Simplicity is an act of will to reduce the fracturedness of life by centering life around a singleness of purpose. Simplicity is spiritual because it deals intimately with the beliefs and views that lend shape and order to our lives. Simplicity is a discipline because we have to work at it and practice it in order to apply it in our lives.

The first key to simplicity is understanding that it begins with an inward focus and unity. One's life grows into an outward expression of that inner reality. The center of this inward focus for a Christian is our faith relationship with God through the life and example of Jesus Christ. This focus can be expressed in the great commandment to love God and neighbor. Out of devotion and gratitude to God we seek to change outwardly. To do so we must intentionally act in ways to foster growth, leaving old ways of being, doing, and thinking.

Simplicity can be an ideal avenue to growth because simplicity involves a deliberate organization of life for a purpose. Without a focused center we are tossed about by the tides and winds of our cultural time. We are distracted by all the things we have and all that we are trying to be. Oftentimes we are possessed by our possessions. Simplicity means being honest and sincere with ourselves about what really matters. It means having a single purpose focused in our faith and avoiding whatever is irrelevant, distracting, or cluttering. This singleness of purpose allows us to become fully the unique human being God created us to be and to live in harmony—shalom—with the rest of creation, to live a life of love. Simplicity requires distinguishing between our needs and wants, and between our habitual patterns of behavior and our choices at each moment.

Simplicity means to encounter life more directly, fully, and wholeheartedly. Here is where we so often miss the boat in matters of faith. We do not seek direct encounters with life or with our faith each day. We don't look for God in the commonplace, in the routine of our daily lives. To do this requires self-reflection, conscious knowledge of ourselves, and attunement to our daily lives. We cannot live in the past or the future and be attuned to the present moment. *Now* is really the only time in which we can live. The past has already happened; the future is yet to be.

Reflection: What are the things that you most value? What are your priorities in daily living? Write your reflection here.

Prayer: Lord Jesus, help us not to run from life, not to try to control it, not get carried away responding to it. Help us, Lord, to realize life is a gift and to encounter life today in this very moment intentionally and consciously. Amen.

DAY TWO

LIVING IN THE PRESENT

Scripture: *And while they went to buy it, the bridegroom came, and those who were ready went with him into the wedding banquet; and the door was shut.*

—Matthew 25:10

The second important element of simplicity is understanding that if we choose to pursue it and embrace it, it will have to be an intentional activity that takes place in the *now*. We can live life more fully when we are aware of it and present to it. Living in the now takes intentional effort. I find myself to be a Christian in great need of grace! I was raised to be performance-oriented, and not only do I need great amounts of grace to achieve the tasks I am given or assume, but I also need lots of grace to chill out and just *be*. After all, God created us as human *beings,* not as human *doings.* For most of us, our lives demand a significant amount of doing, but simplicity can give us a sense of balance between being and doing. When we are present to what it is we are doing or being, living is a richer, fuller experience.

The truth is that much of the time most of us run on automatic, either responding to life or trying to control life and make it go our way. We really are not available to live in the present moment because we do not approach life as a daily adventure, open to whatever God brings our way. I do not know who originated the saying but I like its message: "Now is a gift. That is why it is called the present!"

The inward focus of simplicity must begin in this present moment and for a

Christian, in God's inclusive, universal love covenant. Without the inward, present focus, our decisions will be swayed by other considerations, and we will spend our time, energy, and money responding and controlling life rather than consciously encountering life.

By embracing simplicity we seek a compassionate approach to life that restores shalom and requires integration, balance, justice, and peace in all areas of our lives. Because we understand that we live in a relationship with God, we know that God is present with us in each moment. Thus the act of entrusting ourselves to God's provision and love requires that we live in the present moment. So enjoy today and begin to make a habit of enjoying each day more fully by engaging in it more completely.

Today just concentrate on living. Be aware of what it is you are doing throughout the day. To this end here are two exercises, one involving more *doing* and the other more *being*.

> *Exercise One: Pay attention to each thing that you do today, be it cooking, washing dishes, going to the bank, working at a computer, reading, watching the news, exercising, playing with your pet. Be present to what it is you are doing.*
>
> *Can you enjoy the dishes you are washing rather than wishing the task were over so you could get on to something else? If you are outdoors, what is the weather like? What season of the year is it? What do you smell? What sounds do you hear? If you are driving a car, do you enjoy driving? What do you like about it? How do you feel doing it? Do the other people and cars around you seem to be in a big hurry?*

> *Exercise Two: Even if your day is filled with lots of unavoidable doing, pick sabbaths of time (maybe only three to five minutes) in which you can be rather than do. One of my favorite spiritual authors is the Jesuit priest Thomas Green. He offers an analogy that has empowered me to yield to God's grace. Green used this analogy to explain prayer*

when God did not seem present. Here is my expanded adaptation: Floating on water is a difficult thing for many people, not because it demands a lot of skill but because it demands a lot of "letting go."[1] The secret is in not responding instinctively and getting rigid but relaxing. Imagine that you are resting your head on the water as though on a pillow and don't try to hold it out of the water. Then let the waves carry you. The analogy is simply this: we tend to be swimmers in life when God is really calling us to be floaters on God's sea of life. We want to be in control of our lives and our time and so does God! God is the sea, and God is asking us to trust enough to relax and let God lead us. During the day we have many things to do, and yet if we want to be fully present to whatever moment we are living in, we need to just relax and yield ourselves to the moment and to God's presence.

If you are a water person, when you get your sabbath moments, imagine surrendering yourself to God in the present moment by floating on God's sea of life. Relax and trust God and God's love for you. Now be aware of what it is simply to be alive in God's world.

If the water image does not work for you, then get comfortable, take a few deep breaths, and relax, yielding yourself to God and to the present moment. Be aware of what it is like to be alive. Enjoy!

Prayer: *O Lord our God, maker of the land and sea and all that is, we praise you for the beauty of your creative work. Help us to relax and enjoy that which you have made. Help us to give ourselves over to your loving care—to relax and let you lead us into the fullness of the present moment. Amen.*

DAY THREE

FREE FOR THE ABUNDANT LIFE

Scripture: For six years you shall sow your land and gather in its yield; but the seventh year you shall let it rest and lie fallow, so that the poor of your people may eat; and what they leave the wild animals may eat. You shall do the same with your vineyard, and with your olive orchard.

—*Exodus 23:10-11*

Why are we so possessed by our possessions? Why is it that money—mammon—is such a god in our lives? Part of the answer is cultural, but a significant part of the answer is spiritual. It is a question of priorities in our lives. If we don't have a focus for our lives, our priorities are volatile. They are susceptible to the influences around us. If God is our spiritual center and focus, then we are free to live the abundant life to which Jesus calls us. The passage from John 10:9-10 speaks to this: "I am the gate. Whoever enters by me will be saved, and will come in and go out and find pasture. The thief comes only to steal and kill and destroy. I came that they may have life, and have it abundantly."

Our call is to abundant life, but our enemy would deprive us of such life. When what we have and what we are seeking after drain our time, energy, and monies, we miss the fullness and joy of living. We tend to run around distracted, fractured, running on automatic, so it is no wonder that we don't feel complete or whole. We are not living in God's shalom. Our habits perpetuate this cycle. Let me explain more fully by giving an example.

Mary is called into her boss's office and offered a promotion. A promotion translates to more power, influence, and money. Mary responds to these desirable triggers by accepting the new position. She goes home, shares the good news with her family, and they all go out and celebrate. A few months down the road, however, there is not a great deal of joy in Mary's home. She now has to commute an hour longer each day, which she hates. She misses her old office and friends. Her husband has to pick up the children. Dinner is late every night. The whole family is crabby.

Mary was enticed into the new position by the lure of money, power, and position. She failed to think about *who* she is, what her needs are, as well as the needs of her family. Money, success, and power defined the bottom line, the stimulus to which she automatically responded. She was not truly free in making her decision. She was not really aware or reflective in making her decision. If she had been centered by faith in God, she would have sought guidance and discernment. She would have realized the job's benefits did not exceed the job's drawbacks, and she would have been free to say no to the job offer.

Many of us struggle unsuccessfully to keep God at the center of our daily life so that our discipleship is the core issue in our decisions. As a result we respond to a whole series of triggers that are less than ideal and that keep us subservient to mammon rather than the God of steadfast love and life. Simplicity can help us focus on the one treasure of great value, our relationship with God.

Reflection: *Reflect on the decisions you have made in the last year or so. Where was God or your faith in the decision processes? Would you say that you are fractured, distracted, and running on automatic? Write your reflection here.*

Prayer: *Dear Jesus, help us put on the brakes and slow down. Help us to live in the present time, blessed and enriched by our faith and not responding to a bunch of lesser external triggers. For it is in your name that we pray. Amen.*

DAY FOUR

FAITH

Scripture: I have heard of your faith in the Lord Jesus and your love toward all the saints, and for this reason I do not cease to give thanks for you as I remember you in my prayers.

—*Ephesians 1:15-16*

Everyone has faith—a set of beliefs that reflect our understanding of life. Healthy Christian faith leads us to the shalom God intends for us—a sense of wholeness and harmony. This faith organizes life around our true center, our true self.

Faith is complex. It encompasses *action, content,* and *witness.*

The *action* faith initially requires is accepting God's love for us. That acceptance leads to our repentance, our assurance of receiving forgiveness, and our believing the good news. Faith is not merely a belief in ideas or concepts but a belief that moves us to action. The New Testament usage of *faith* derives largely from the Hebrew understanding that "to believe" is to have firmness, reliability, or steadfastness.[2] Faith in action is a steadfast trusting in God and in our relationship with God.

Faith has substance or *content.* By this I mean values, beliefs, promises, and all that comprises the "good news." Faith's content performs the crucial function of integrating the different aspects of our lives by providing an overarching purpose or meaning.

A significant part of our faith is how we live it out daily, for our actions and our lifestyles witness to the true faith we hold. Somehow in our upbringing, many Western Christians have missed the critical link between faith and lifestyle. Faith should express itself in what we eat, how we spend our time, how we entertain ourselves, and how we spend our money. There must be a connection between our faith and our daily economic habits. We as a Christian people need to grow in our faith in order to bridge the gap between faith actions, faith beliefs, and faith lifestyles or witness.

For faith to grow, we must be open and listening to God through scripture, prayer, worship, music, nature, people, and the circumstances of our lives. Then we must be obedient to God's will and direction for us as we discern them. True Christian faith leads us to involvement with others and sensitivity to their needs.

Active faith in our relationship with God and God's covenant relationship with the world require that we rest in the trust of God's provision and live more fully in the present moment. If we trust God's provision, we will be more generous with what we have. We will not feel the need to hoard. Rather we can pass on our blessings. Economic simplicity is a stance of generosity toward others—a willingness to reduce one's own blessings in order to meet the needs of others. A life of simplicity usually does not happen overnight. To embrace simplicity means working out one's salvation by striving to be in the world but not of the world.

Most of us have to come under a dual conviction in order to change. First, we must be under the conviction that the wrong values are guiding our lives; second, we must be under the conviction that shalom and love are deeper values that should be guiding our lives. By virtue of being Christian, we have love and shalom at the heart of our covenantal relationship with life, and we should express these in our daily living. To say that more directly: Our lifestyle reflects whether or not we are living out of our Christian faith. Jesus said, "For where your treasure is, there your heart will be also" (Matthew 6:21). Because we exist within the deceptiveness of the addictive process, most of us lie to ourselves and to others. We may characterize ourselves and our relationships in one way, but the reality of our behavior reflects a different picture—a different witness. How we spend our time, money, and energies reflects the values we live by.

Think of exercising your faith as analogous to rowing a boat. If you use only one oar, what happens? You go in circles. If the life of faith is like rowing a boat, one oar would be the *content* of what you believe, while the other would be the expression of that belief—the witness, the action. If you are all belief and no action, you will go in circles. If you are all action and no belief, you will go in a circle. The energy to move both oars comes from authentic love.

> *Reflection:* What does rowing with both oars mean in your spiritual journey? Think about some particular instances when you may have used only one oar and what happened. What would it mean to use two oars? Write your reflection here.

> *Prayer:* O Jesus, comforter of our souls, show us that genuine faith must be reflected in our daily lifestyles. Help us to express our faith in ways to which you particularly call us. Amen.

DAY FIVE

TRAITS OF SIMPLICITY

Scripture: My child, if you accept my words and treasure up my commandments within you, making your ear attentive to wisdom and inclining your heart to understanding; if you indeed cry out for insight, and raise your voice for understanding; if you seek it like silver, and search for it as for hidden treasures—then you will understand the fear of the Lord and find the knowledge of God.

—Proverbs 2:1-5

Being made in the image of God demands a link between the fidelity of a caring God and our own ethical interpersonal behavior, making moral choices between goods and evils. To reflect this link requires a relationship between faith and our lifestyle, especially our daily economic choices. As a spiritual discipline, simplicity focuses us on our Divine Creator. Our spiritual reality can inform and enlighten the physical reality of the world around us. Neither reality is separate, but both are parts of the same, whole reality. Our lives are not compartmentalized but lived holistically.

Richard Foster provides a list of traits associated with a vow or commitment to simplicity:[3]

- unity of heart and singleness of purpose
- joy in God's good creation and free gifts
- contentment and trust
- freedom from covetousness

- modesty and temperance in all things
- grateful receipt of material provision
- using money without abusing money
- availability to serve God full-time
- giving joyfully and generously

Remember that habits take a long time to become rooted. I have spent a lifetime growing addictive and compulsive spending habits, but each time I resist the temptation to buy unnecessary things, I strengthen in the habit of resisting and weaken the habit of spending.

What is perhaps harder than breaking habits in daily economic choices is coming to terms with the real human cost of our consumption. Kenneth Boulding offers two metaphors for understanding our economy of the past and of the present. In the past we had a "cowboy" economy in which we could exploit an apparently limitless and underdeveloped planet.[4] Through the cowboy's eyes there was enough for anyone who would work hard enough to get it. We have now entered the time of the "spaceman" economy in which the earth is a single spaceship with limited resources. As humans we are forced to find our place in a cyclical ecological system. Now there is enough for everyone's need but not enough for everyone's greed. Considering that 30 percent of the world's population receives 70 percent of the world's income and resources, something has got to change, and that something is the set of rules and games that govern economic life.

By God's grace I hope to remember and live by the truth that simplicity in economics is not a choice for a true Christian. Once we choose for God, we have indeed made our choice!

Reflection: Are you willing to grow in simplicity—in your focus on God, your transformation to Christlikeness, and your wise and generous economic stewardship? Write your reflection here.

Prayer: Almighty God, grant us each the grace to transform into the loving people we are created to be. Amen.

GROUP SESSION

LIVING SIMPLICITY

Opening Prayer

Giving God, you have blessed us with fullness of life. Help us to let you transform that fullness into the abundance that comes from centering ourselves in you and in your love. Help us to be still and know who you are. Help us to be still and know who we are. Help us to be still and know who others are. Amen.

Activity (Allow five minutes.)

Have the group divide into pairs. Let the partners share with each other in what ways each person feels he or she is like Martha or like Mary (Luke 10:40-42, the scripture for this week).

Discussion (Allow fifteen minutes.)

Divide into groups of three or four and discuss the following questions.

1. How would you define the simplicity expressed by Jesus' life? Give biblical examples to support your view.
2. Jesus said, "Do not worry about tomorrow, for tomorrow will bring worry of its own. Today's trouble is enough for today" (Matthew 6:34). How might this relate to the concept that simplicity requires living in the present moment?

In the large group, share the highlights from each group.

Activity (Allow fifteen minutes.)

Let the group sit silently for several minutes. Then have members think back on their week's activities. Do the activities reflect a self-serving faith or an authentic Christ-centered faith? Let each person consider the question "What can you do during the next week to connect your faith and your lifestyle?" Have each person turn to his or her neighbor to share the answer.

Discussion (Allow twenty minutes.)

Returning to the small groups, discuss this question: If simplicity involves focusing on your faith as the guiding light of your life, where do family, work, church, pleasure, and other aspects of your life fit?

Optional question

If time allows, discuss the traits of simplicity listed on Day One of this week. Which are most meaningful to you and why?

Closing

Form a circle and offer thanksgiving for the blessings of ordinary daily life. Especially lift up things you were mindful of this past week. Go away filled with the blessings of life.

WEEK FOUR

Zacchaeus stood there and said to the Lord, "Look, half of my posses-
sions, Lord, I will give to the poor; and if I have defrauded anyone of
anything, I will pay back four times as much." Then Jesus said to him,
"Today salvation has come to this house, because he too is a son of
Abraham. For the Son of Man came to seek out and to save the lost."

—*Luke 19:8-10*

GOD'S POSITION TOWARD THE POOR

Scripture: *If you lend money to my people, to the poor among you, you shall not deal with them as a creditor; you shall not exact interest from them.*

—Exodus 22:25

There is a lot of talk these days that God is on the side of the poor and that as followers of Christ we should take the same stance. To understand the overall view of God's position toward the poor and the rich, we will look first at God's actions in the pivotal points of history—the Exodus, the destruction of Israel and Judah, and the Incarnation.

God's covenant with Abraham is one of enormous blessing. The covenant becomes communal when God frees Jacob's offspring from slavery in Egypt. In the Exodus the Almighty displays power to free economically and politically oppressed slaves, as well as to maintain the covenant with Abraham. Following the Exodus from Egypt, the Holy One gives Israel the law. This covenant gift is encapsulated in the Ten Commandments whose preamble identifies God as the One who brought Israel out of the land of Egypt (Deuteronomy 5:6; Exodus 20:2), and thus the One who has first claim on each person's life. The Ten Commandments reflect the community's covenant with God and with one another, establishing boundaries on human behavior that foster lives pleasing to God and healthy for humans. There can be no adultery, murder, coveting, stealing, and so on among people if they are to live together in shalom.

Although God's covenant and law set constraints on how the people could live together in peace and justice, the people chose to disobey. According to the prophets Amos, Hosea, Isaiah, Micah, and Jeremiah, God destroyed Israel because of idolatry and mistreatment of the poor. Based on the sizes of houses uncovered, archaeologists have confirmed that a shocking discrepancy between the rich and the poor existed by the middle of the eighth century B.C.E. when Amos announced that the Northern Kingdom of Israel would be destroyed. Why destroyed? Because the rich trample the poor into the dust (Amos 2:7); the affluent lifestyle of the rich is built on the oppression of the poor (Amos 6:1-7); the rich women oppress the poor and crush the needy (Amos 4:1); and the rich bribe the judges so even in the courts the poor have no hope (Amos 5:10-15). Hosea, Amos's contemporary, disclosed the nation's idolatry as the other critical cause in the impending destruction (Hosea 8:1-6; 9:1-3).

As for the Southern Kingdom of Judah, Isaiah addressed the people as "you who make iniquitous decrees, . . . to turn aside the needy from justice and to rob the poor of my people of their right" (Isaiah 10:1-2), and warned that this mistreatment of the poor would bring about their destruction. Micah also denounced Judah, whose people "covet fields, and seize them; and houses, and take them away; they oppress a man and his house, a man and his inheritance" (Micah 2:2 RSV). After a reprisal, one hundred years later Jeremiah again brought God's judgment against the people for injustice and idolatry.

God's passion for justice is a two-edged sword. When Israel was oppressed, they were freed; when Israel became the oppressor, they were destroyed. God remains on the side of the poor regardless of who the oppressor is.

For Christians the Incarnation is the most pivotal historical event—God dwelling with humanity in Jesus Christ. Jesus is the definitive revelation of God's nature. In the New Testament the Gospel of Luke finds Jesus beginning his public ministry in the synagogue at Nazareth with the words of the prophet Isaiah:

> The Spirit of the Lord is upon me, because he has anointed me to bring good
> news to the poor. He has sent me to proclaim release to the captives and

recovery of sight to the blind, to let the oppressed go free, to proclaim the year of the Lord's favor. (Luke 4:18-19; compare Isaiah 61:1-2)

In this text, Jesus singles out only one group as the recipients of his gospel, the poor. In his ministry Jesus liberated people from both physical and *material* problems. Jesus fed the hungry as well as healing the blind and sick. And indeed the judgment passage in the Gospel of Matthew suggests that failure literally to feed the hungry, to clothe the naked, or to visit the prisoners will lead to eternal damnation (Matthew 25:31-46).

God not only acts in history to liberate the poor, but God also expresses in scripture an identification with the poor that we can only partially fathom. The Book of Proverbs states simply, "Those who oppress the poor insult their Maker, but those who are kind to the needy honor him," and "Whoever is kind to the poor lends to the Lord, and will be repaid in full" (Proverbs 14:31; 19:17). God's identification with the poor is expressed most completely by Jesus' words in the judgment story:

> Come, you that are blessed by my Father, inherit the kingdom prepared for you from the foundation of the world; for I was hungry and you gave me food, I was thirsty and you gave me something to drink, I was a stranger and you welcomed me, I was naked and you gave me clothing, I was sick and you took care of me, I was in prison and you visited me. Then the righteous will answer him, "Lord, when was it that we saw you hungry and gave you food, or thirsty and gave you something to drink? And when was it that we saw you a stranger and welcomed you, or naked and gave you clothing? And when was it that we saw you sick or in prison and visited you?" And the king will answer them, "Truly I tell you, just as you did it to one of the least of these who are members of my family, you did it to me." (Matthew 25:34-40)

Those who did not care for the needy neighbors are cursed to eternal fire. God, as revealed in Jesus Christ, clearly identifies with the least of people. When we do or do not do unto the least, we do unto God.

The poor, the illiterate, the drug addict, and the criminal offend most of us. Yet scripture says when we respond to them we are responding to God. If we are repulsed and respond in kind, so we have responded to God. If we are repulsed but overcome that reaction by grace and respond in genuine love, so we have responded to God.

Reflection: Reflect today on how you respond to the people in your world. Do some repulse you? Which ones? How do you deal with your automatically negative responses to people? Write your reflection here.

Exercise: Practice seeing God in someone who seems "unlovable" to you today.

Prayer: O Jesus, each person is precious and equal in your sight. Give us the empowering grace to see you in others and to respond in compassion—to encourage and nurture each individual as you would have us do. Amen.

GOD EXALTS THE POOR

Scripture: If you take your neighbor's cloak in pawn, you shall restore it before the sun goes down; for it may be your neighbor's only clothing to use as cover; in what else shall that person sleep? And if your neighbor cries out to me, I will listen, for I am compassionate.

—Exodus 22:26-27

While God called Abraham as an individual leader, God's first significant act toward the chosen people as a whole was the Exodus. In choosing the Hebrew people, God chose to work through poor slaves from Egypt rather than a wealthy nation. Similarly, Jesus is born not to a Sadducean family but to a carpenter who has to offer two pigeons rather than a lamb at Jesus' purification rite (Luke 2:24; see Leviticus 12:6-8). With the exception of Matthew, Jesus' chosen disciples appear to be fishermen and other common folk. And the early church consisted predominantly of poor people. Paul writes:

> Consider your own call, brothers and sisters: not many of you were wise by human standards, not many were powerful, not many were of noble birth. But God chose what is foolish in the world to shame the wise; God chose what is weak in the world to shame the strong; God chose what is low and despised in the world, things that are not, to reduce to nothing things that are, so that no one might boast in the presence of God. (1 Corinthians 1:26-29)

This passage highlights the difference between God's procedures and ours. If we want to make something happen, we go to the people whom we believe have the greatest power and influence. This is not so with God. The Creator picks slaves, prostitutes, carpenters, and fishermen to save the world. God always seems to be in the business of inverting our social standards and order.

Two powerful scriptural texts uphold this theme, Mary's Magnificat and Jesus' Beatitudes. In the first, Mary proclaims to Elizabeth: "My soul magnifies the Lord . . . . He has brought down the powerful from their thrones, and lifted up the lowly; he has filled the hungry with good things, and sent the rich away empty" (Luke 1:46, 52-53; see 1 Samuel 2:2-8, Song of Hannah). Similarly in the Beatitudes the poor are lifted up and the rich cursed:

> Blessed are you who are poor, for yours is the kingdom of God. Blessed are you who are hungry now, for you will be filled . . . . But woe to you who are rich, for you have received your consolation. Woe to you who are full now, for you will be hungry. (Luke 6:20-21, 24-25)

The Beatitudes form part of the Sermon on the Plain (known as the Sermon on the Mount in Matthew), which is crucial to understanding Jesus' teaching. Again God is inverting the normal human way of doing business.

To understand God's concern for the poor and oppressed is not enough. Scripture specifically commands believers to imitate God's special concern for them. In the Hebrew Scriptures God reminds Israel of their former oppression,

> You shall not wrong or oppress a resident alien, for you were aliens in the land of Egypt. You shall not abuse any widow or orphan. If you do abuse them, when they cry out to me, I will surely heed their cry; my wrath will burn, and I will kill you with the sword, and your wives shall become widows and your children orphans. (Exodus 22:21-24)

Widows, orphans, and strangers receive particular attention, each meriting about forty verses commanding justice for them. Equal justice for the poor in court is another consistent concern. In fact, it is the law: "You shall not pervert the justice due to your poor in their lawsuits" (Exodus 23:6).

In the New Testament, Jesus commands followers to show bias to the poor:

> When you give a luncheon or a dinner, do not invite your friends or your brothers or your relatives or rich neighbors, in case they may invite you in return, and you would be repaid. But when you give a banquet, invite the poor, the crippled, the lame, and the blind. And you will be blessed, because they cannot repay you, for you will be repaid at the resurrection of the righteous. (Luke 14:12-14)

The Gospel of Luke reports Jesus' teaching to imitate God's mercy in lending:

> If you do good to those who do good to you, what credit is that to you? For even sinners do the same. If you lend to those from whom you hope to receive, what credit is that to you? Even sinners lend to sinners, to receive as much again. But love your enemies, do good, and lend, expecting nothing in return. (Luke 6:33-35)

Luke sums up this imperative for mercy by recording Jesus' command, "Be merciful, just as your Father is merciful" (Luke 6:36). Our hearts are to be after God's own heart.

An honest appraisal of scripture shows without a doubt that God does have a special concern for the poor and that we are called to have the same concern. Does this mean that God disapproves of or dislikes the rich? No. Abraham, Moses, Paul, Zacchaeus, Luke, and Lydia are examples of wealthy, educated people through whom God works. To say that God is on the side of the poor does not mean God is biased; nor does it mean material poverty is a biblical ideal. Certainly God does not overlook the sins of the poor because they are poor. But God is not neutral toward the poor either. God is on the side of the poor because throughout biblical history more often than not the poor are neglected or oppressed by the rich. The poor have special vulnerability; hence God is at work casting down the rich and exalting the poor.

Vulnerability is the significant word here. God's design is always for us to share in God's compassion and mercy. I doubt that anything delights God more than our loving care for those who are in a vulnerable position. What is important in our actions is the motivation behind them. If we give aid to Kosovo refugees out of compassion, this act greatly pleases God. If we give aid with the aim of getting a soliciting relative off our back, this act, devoid of love, is empty of meaning.

Most of us pay taxes every year to aid the vulnerable in our country. How would it affect us to think of this "giving" as a compassionate act toward those who have been less fortunate than we have been? That perspective might ease the pain of giving and actually open our hearts to greater generosity! It is something worth thinking about.

Reflection: As a member of a wealthy country seeking a faithful connection between your faith and your economic lifestyle, ask yourself these questions: Are we wealthy at the expense of others? Are we truly giving to help more needy people? Write your reflection here.

Prayer: O Jesus, your love knew no bounds as you willingly sacrificed your own life for our betterment. Touch our hearts this day with your compassion. Empower us by your grace to be loving agents of your grace to others. Help us to act and to work for the betterment of those less fortunate than ourselves. It is in your name we pray. Amen.

DAY THREE

CONVERSION AND SALVATION

Scripture: Like newborn infants, long for the pure, spiritual milk, so that by it you may grow into salvation—if indeed you have tasted that the Lord is good.

—*1 Peter 2:2-3*

It is helpful to distinguish between conversion and salvation. Conversion marks the beginning of the salvation process; it is the act of repentance, a turning away from sin and self-motivated, self-preoccupied ways of being and toward God's will and way. The act of conversion requires obedience to God. Jesus' call to conversion requires repentance and belief: "The time is fulfilled, and the kingdom of God has come near; repent, and believe in the good news" (Mark 1:15). We not only grieve for and turn from our misdeeds, but we actually accept God's gift of faith.

Salvation on the other hand is the ongoing development of that gift of faith. Salvation is the work of God, and there is an aspect of salvation that is and always will be mysterious. Here are some characteristics we can discern from scripture. In both the Old and New Testaments salvation implies deliverance *from* threat or danger or oppression *to* something. Consider Israel's deliverance from slavery in Egypt. It was salvation *from* oppression *to* a covenant community that would become the vessel for salvation for all the peoples of the earth. We may think of salvation in any number of biblical metaphors and images, such as being called *from* darkness *into* God's light (1 Peter 2:9), *from* slavery *to* freedom (Galatians 5:1), *from* being subjects *to* being children of God (Galatians 3:25-26). I have always been intrigued with Paul's instruction to "work out your own salvation with fear and trembling" (Philippians 2:12). For Paul salvation is not a one-time act but rather a process that one works out and that requires obedience. Paul's is certainly not an isolated view of salvation. Consider the words of 1 Peter 2:2 above, "so that by it you may grow into salvation."

Though the New Testament displays many facets of salvation, all definitions carry a strong moral content. A moral shift is part of being saved *from* something *to* something different. Consider Ephesians 2:8-10: "For by grace you have been saved through faith . . . created in Christ Jesus for good works, which God prepared beforehand to be our way of life." We have been freed *from* sin and death *for* good works. We are not just called to "works" but to "good works." Israel was not to be just a community but to be one that imaged God in the way they lived with God and with one another.

Salvation is not simply a personal experience, a "me-and-Jesus" thing. When Zacchaeus experienced salvation in the presence of Jesus, that change immediately affected all who touched his world. He would repay any that he had defrauded, and he would give half of all he had to the poor. Not for one minute do I think Zacchaeus then returned to his old ways, living isolated from Jesus' followers. Rather like the early Christians in the Book of Acts, he would have sought the fellowship of like-minded souls to remember the words of Jesus, to do works of compassion and justice, and to pray.

Growth into salvation affects us personally, socially, and politically. Conversion in each area helps us to develop a balanced spirituality necessary for living in God's intended shalom. This experience of conversion in different areas is best expressed by the prophet Micah: "He has told you, O mortal, what is good; and what does the Lord require of you but to do justice, and to love kindness, and to walk humbly with your God?" (Micah 6:8). To grow in salvation ideally we need to experience conversion in each of three areas.

The *personal conversion* is the one we normally associate with the word *conversion*. It is an experience when the realness of God breaks in upon our lives, generating a sense of God's love, care, and providence. This experience reflects Micah's words "to walk humbly with your God."

Our experience of God's presence and provision cannot end with us because God's acts of creation and covenant cause all humankind to be interrelated. So the next conversion is in the *social* dimension, involving genuine interest in other people, love for our neighbors. This social dimension can be linked to Micah's phrase "to love kindness." Social conversion requires openness, listening to others, as well as entrusting ourselves to them. A lifestyle reflective of our positive faith is the outcome of social conversion.

The third area for conversion is *political* and relates to Micah's call to "do justice." A political conversion means not just a change of heart but a real change in one's outlook regarding how society is organized; how wealth, power, privileges, rights, and responsibilities are distributed at every level—local, national, and global. The call to act justly requires understanding how society works and committing to correct injustices. Few of us get involved in the political area, but responsible citizenship, voting, and voicing concerns to government representatives are steps in the right direction.

In both the deliverance of Israel from Egypt and the covenant on Sinai, the whole community was involved. Israel as a community was delivered *from* oppression *to* become a covenanted community of mutual responsibility. In a similar way, drawing *from* Old Testament roots, the early church was shaped *into* a people of God with a global mission. Mutual responsibility in a community faith was a theme from Pentecost to Paul's concern to gather provisions for the Jerusalem church, from the local care of widows to the commission to go into all the world.

Reflection: *What are some consequences of understanding salvation as a lifelong process rather than a single act? Many people think conversion applies only to individuals. What might happen if you and members of your church experienced a social or political conversion? Write your reflection here.*

Prayer: *O Savior dear, how easy we want to make salvation—a simple decision or two! Help us to recognize the true nature of salvation and to desire it with all our heart. Amen.*

DAY FOUR

JESUS' RESPONSE TO POVERTY

Scripture: *Take care! Be on your guard against all kinds of greed; for one's life does not consist in the abundance of possessions.*

—*Luke 12:15*

Though neither the church nor Christians often advertise it, Jesus was quite clear on the issue of economics. Put simply, Jesus believed that surplus wealth should be used to aid the poor.

The Gospel of Luke particularly is concerned with the relationship between the wealthy and the poor. Jesus identifies the audience of his ministry as the poor from the time he teaches in the synagogue at Nazareth, reading these words of the prophet Isaiah, "The Spirit of the Lord is upon me, because he has anointed me to bring good news to the poor." Both Jesus' teachings and his actions affirm his concern for the poor. Let's look at several examples of Jesus' teachings.

First, Jesus is opposed to the accumulation of possessions. In the scripture for today, Luke 12:15, Jesus cautions against covetousness and then tells the parable of the rich fool who built more barns to handle his excess harvest. In the parable there is no criticism of the rich man except that he kept the additional goods for himself and did not use them to be "rich toward God" (12:21). It is good to be blessed, but it is damning to fail to be generous toward God by sharing with the needy. Similarly Jesus counsels the rich to give to the poor. When the rich young ruler asks Jesus what he must do to inherit eternal life, Jesus responds, "Sell all that you own and distribute the money to the poor, and you will have treasure in heaven; then come, follow me" (Luke 18:22). This theme is not a stray brush stroke in Luke's composition of a picture of Jesus. In Luke 12:33 Jesus calls his followers to "sell your possessions, and give alms." And in Luke 6:30, 35 Jesus says, "Give to everyone who begs from you; and if anyone takes away your goods, do not ask for them again . . . . But love your enemies, do good, and lend, expecting nothing in return." These are tough words for materialistic people of today's Western world to hear.

Jesus teaches his disciples to reduce their anxiety toward possessions by embracing a life of material simplicity. In Luke 12:22-34 we find this teaching:

> Therefore I tell you, do not worry about your life, what you will eat, or about your body, what you will wear. For life is more than food, and the body more than clothing. Consider the ravens: . . . yet God feeds them. Of how much more value are you than the birds! And can any of you by worrying add a single hour to your span of life? If then you are not able to do so small a thing as that, why do you worry about the rest? Consider the lilies, . . . how much more will he clothe you—you of little faith! And do not keep striving for what you are to eat and what you are to drink, and do not keep worrying. For it is the nations of the world that strive after all these things, and your Father knows that you need them. Instead, strive for his kingdom, and these things will be given to you as well. . . . Sell your possessions, and give alms. Make purses for yourselves that do not wear out, an unfailing treasure in heaven, where no thief comes near and no moth destroys. For where your treasure is, there your heart will be also.

If we have the kingdom of God as our central focus in life, everything we need will be provided. Does this mean none of us will ever lack for anything? No. Birds do starve to death, as do humans. But the promise is that God's presence with us will be enough. Worry gains us nothing. Trust in God gains us everything. We can do or endure all things through Christ who gives us strength! Again, where our treasure is, there our heart will be. We must focus on the kingdom to be freed from our material life.

Second, while Jesus accepts hospitality from the rich and works miracles among them, he also criticizes them. He says, "Woe to you who are rich, for you have received your consolation. Woe to you who are full now, for you will be hungry" (Luke 6:24-25). But this criticism also is punctuated by the story of the rich man and the poor beggar (Luke 16:19-31). There is a direct relationship between the rich man's fate and his refusal to share his possessions with the poor man at his gate. The contrast between rich and poor is heightened when Jesus later compares the temple offering from the wealthy men who "contributed out of their abundance" with the poor widow who gave "out of her poverty," putting in "all she had to live on" (Luke 21:4).

Third, Jesus praises those who give up their possessions to help the poor. The most important encounter is that with Zacchaeus, who embraces Jesus' teachings about his surplus possessions. In response to Jesus' presence in his home, Zacchaeus gives half of his goods to the poor. Jesus comments on this act by saying, "Today salvation has come to this house" (Luke 19:9). The story of Zacchaeus stands in stark contrast to the story of the rich young ruler. In accepting Jesus' teachings regarding possessions and making the kingdom first in his life, Zacchaeus joins the ranks of Jesus' faithful disciples who have heard Jesus' words and put them into practice in their lives.

In the Gospel of Luke we find a wealth of instruction from Jesus on how to behave toward others in the economic realm. Most important is to practice simplicity by focusing our heart on God and God's kingdom, for that will lead to proper priorities and a spirit of generosity.

Reflection: *In what ways do you share with others (sharing includes giving support and hlep to family members as well as needy strangers)? Write your reflection here.*

Prayer: *Precious Lord, we love our treasured possessions for they define and comfort us. Help us to put you first, to have or have not according to your desires. Amen.*

DAY FIVE

SANCTIFYING FAITH

Scripture: *Therefore, do not let sin exercise dominion in your mortal bodies, to make you obey their passions. No longer present your members to sin as instruments of wickedness, but present yourselves to God as those who have been brought from death to life, and present your members to God as instruments of righteousness.*

—*Romans 6:12-13*

If I understand Paul correctly, we are going to be slaves to something. We are going to act in obedience either to the selfish desires that rise up within us or we are going to present ourselves to God for God's good purpose to be worked out in our lives. Paul puts it bluntly, "You have been freed from sin and enslaved to God" (Romans 6:22). We who pride ourselves on our independence and self-sufficiency (or at least the illusion of independence and self-sufficiency!) find the idea of being "enslaved to God" hard to swallow. But the call of the gospel, the call of Christ, has always been to give up our life to embrace his, to pick up our cross and follow him.

Healthy faith is organized around a true center, allowing integration of the individual life, as well as integration of one's life with the rest of society and creation. In order to have and to grow in a healthy, mature faith, we need a great abundance of God's grace. That grace does in us what we cannot do for ourselves. God gives us this grace through sanctification. *Sanctification* is the process of transforming our lives; it is the work of the Holy Spirit within us (Romans 15:16; 1 Peter 1:2) after our personal conversion to the power and presence of God in our lives. Sanctification perfects us in the image of Jesus Christ and develops us as the people God created us to be, living in shalom with God, others, and creation.

Now sanctification sounds good, but do we really want to be perfected in the image of God, to grow into the likeness of Jesus Christ? Do we really want to live in shalom with others? Do we really want to pay the price? Are we willing to send our kingdoms away in order that "God's kingdom might come" in our lives? These are painful and difficult questions.

It is important to understand that sanctification is not about change but about transformation. *Change* is the process of replacing one thing with another; change frequently is under our control. In contrast, *transformation* is an inner process—God working in us in a way that unfolds beyond our control. In Luke 18 the rich young ruler comes to Jesus wanting to know what he can do to inherit eternal life. The man wants to change, to "do" something to inherit eternal life, but Jesus calls him to a fundamental transformation in his being.

Sanctification takes place as we actively live out of our faith. In the summer of 1999 I took a leap of faith that has brought about transformation, not merely change, in my life. I left my comfortable life as a United Methodist pastor in Oklahoma to move to Austin, Texas. I moved with a vision, a calling to build a retreat center for healing and wholeness in the hill country. There are no clear-cut paths for the fulfillment of this vision; there is no linear flow for me to follow to achieve my dream. There are just the daily paths that cross my life. I came with a vision and a place to live. I also came with a significant amount of indebtedness and no job. Work materialized but in a different way than imagined. My work with Hospice Austin is unsurpassed in personal fulfillment. Nonetheless for the first time as an adult, I make an hourly wage and have no benefits. This status certainly changes my perspective after twenty-five years of salaries and benefits!

This is my second step backward in finances, yet I am stronger in faith than ever. By the grace of God, I do not worry about achieving my retreat center dream but rather accept what each day presents. I am able to make these faith steps and to dwell in peace rather than fear. The daily invitation I experience is to trust God more in all things, including my finances.

Faith and the Holy Spirit are like leaven or seeds within us. As they are nurtured within us they grow, and what takes place in our lives is far more than the changes we effect to reflect our faith. Through God's working in us, we become new creations. Nurturing is vital to sanctification because the process doesn't take place by happenstance but requires our decision to pursue it as well as our discipline, determination, and obedience. Sanctification begins when we embrace the circumstance within which God can bring transformation into our lives. Choosing to be part of this study is an example of placing oneself in a position to be converted. Certainly my writing this study has given God ample opportunity to do radical surgery on my heart!

The biggest obstacle to sanctification is one's own self. To be free from the tyranny of self, we must be free from destructive self-centeredness, deception, and the illusion of control. To be free of the tyranny of self, we must know ourselves better.

Authentic prayer born from a real desire and need will be met by grace that will foster a greater self-knowledge, awareness, and appreciation of what is going on within us. Often I want to buy something I don't really need. In fact I would go so far as to say I am driven to obtain it. Why do I want it so badly, and why must I have it now? Seeking the answer to those two questions in prayer can be very enlightening!

Reflection: Where in your life is the Holy Spirit calling you to change? How does this calling connect with your daily devotional practices? with your economic decisions? Write your reflection here.

Prayer: Lord Jesus, help us to rest in our emptiness so that we can be filled with your presence and grace. Amen.

ROMANS 7

Opening Prayer

Giving God, after our readings this week there can be no doubt in our mind that you desire us to be generous with those less fortunate. And yet even knowing your will, we often find it hard to give freely. Come and touch us now. Move on our hearts to free us to generosity. Help us to support and encourage one another in the path of sanctifying faith. Amen.

Questions

Let the group members compile comments and questions about the week's material and exercises.

Discussion (Allow thirty to thirty-five minutes.)

In addition to questions gathered by the group, consider one or more of the following questions in small groups.

1. What is your understanding of the meanings of conversion and salvation?
2. What was insightful or confusing about this week's lessons?
3. How have this week's lessons helped you to *see* yourself better? to see your calling as a Christian better?

In the large group, share the highlights from each group.

Activity (Allow ten minutes.)

Let one group member read Romans 7:14-25 aloud to the group. Then have group members pair off with a neighbor and discuss this question: How do you respond to situations in which you have failed to do what you wanted—what you knew was right—and instead have done the very things you knew were wrong?

Activity (Allow ten minutes.)

Let group members think for a few minutes about opportunities to serve the poor or vulnerable which have gone unanswered, where their Christian faith has not been put into action. Reflect on these questions: What would enable you to take action? Are you ready to respond in faith where you see the needs of the poor and vulnerable? How could we as Christians support one another in our commitments?

Let the group pair off again and share responses.

Closing

A Meditation Based on the Beatitudes[1]

People who do not hold tightly to things are happy,
   because all of God's kingdom is theirs.
People who are gentle with the earth
   will see it blossom forever.
People who can cry for all the world's suffering,
   will live to see happiness.
People who hunger and thirst for what is right,
   will finally have their fill.
People who really care,
   will find love wherever they go.
People who don't let the world get them down,
   will see God.
People who make peace happen,
   are God's children.
People who give up their own comfort so that others can be helped,
   know what heaven is all about.
LORD, LET US BE LIKE THESE!

PART THREE

—TRANSFORMATION—
COMING DOWN THE
SYCAMORE TREE

Turn my heart to your decrees,
and not to selfish gain.
Turn my eyes from looking at vanities;
give me life in your ways.

—Psalm 119:36-37

WEEK FIVE

READ THE FOLLOWING SCRIPTURE
PASSAGE EACH DAY THIS WEEK.

Work out your own salvation with fear and trembling; for it is God who is at work in you, enabling you both to will and to work for his good pleasure.

—Philippians 2:12-13

DAY ONE

DEADLY SINS

Scripture: For this very reason, you must make every effort to support your faith with goodness, and goodness with knowledge, and knowledge with self-control, and self-control with endurance, and endurance with godliness, and godliness with mutual affection, and mutual affection with love. For if these things are yours and are increasing among you, they keep you from being ineffective and unfruitful in the knowledge of our Lord Jesus Christ.

—2 Peter 1:5-8

Sin is a word we have grown uncomfortable with in recent decades. When I was a child I was taught that we were born with "original sin," the blemish of Adam and Eve's sin in the Garden. The only way to get rid of this sin was the act of baptism. If a person died without being baptized she went to limbo or hell, depending upon her age. Today a growing number of people find baptism unnecessary. Advances in psychology help us understand why we do the things we do, and psychological explanations have replaced our responsibility for the things we do. Understanding part of the "why" of behavior is great, but as Christian people of faith we are responsible and accountable for our actions. Understanding does not replace responsibility.

The simplest way to define sin is: to "miss the mark," to fail to do or be what God calls us to, to break the commandments. As people made in the image of God, we have the ability and the obligation to make moral choices for good in our lives. And sin is not just about doing wrong; it is about boundaries. In Genesis 3 God sets up a boundary for Adam and Eve: they may eat of all the fruit of the garden except that of one tree. Adam and Eve refuse to accept that boundary.

As a child I also was taught about the seven deadly sins—pride, envy, anger, sloth, greed, gluttony, and lust. This list originated with an Eastern monastic movement whose adherents sought to love God with all their hearts and souls and minds. These men and women intentionally withdrew from society in order to purify themselves and live more honestly as Christians. They epitomize worldly renunciation. They took few possessions with them and entered an environment of silence and solitude. Saturated with scripture, they didn't stop with these measures but wanted to know their enemy, who could draw them away from God. So they came up with a list of originating sins, sins that generate other sins, as an aid for them in their spiritual warfare. Between 590–604 C.E. Pope Gregory the Great gave the list its present form.[1]

It is amazing how many of these sins are actively encouraged today: pride, anger, envy, greed, gluttony, and lust. It seems our eyes have been blinded by the dominant culture and institutions into thinking first about ourselves and our desires. Similarly the church encourages our deception by not speaking out against the dominant culture or institutions and by not calling us to a biblical accounting of sin. Our concept of sin is culturally conditioned. Indeed the notion of sin has been all but wiped out by modern psychology. Interestingly Jesus never defined sin. He dealt with the reality of sin, however, calling for repentance and giving his life for our reconciliation. Repentance involves turning from destructive ways toward kingdom ways of being.

The deadly sins are largely boundary sins. Consider these definitions. *Greed* is the excessive desire for acquiring or having; it is a desire for more than one needs. *Envy* is a feeling of discontent or ill will because of another's advantage or possessions. Envy consumes one's own life while one is centered on someone else's life. *Lust* is an intense desire or longing, especially sexual desire. *Gluttony* is excessive eating or greed for food. In each of these sins a natural boundary is being disregarded.

The writer of 2 Peter understood the process necessary to break free from sin. He suggests we make every effort to support our faith with goodness. Each day we make dozens of decisions that either encourage or negate our faith. If we are greedy and take more than our portion, we are negating our faith. If we decide to share, we are living our faith.

These works of goodness must be supported by knowledge. Do our sins of greed, gluttony, envy, or lust affect others? How does what we do hurt others? If we know our greed is hurting our family, then we must support that knowledge with self-control. Once we lose sight of the truth, the blinders of deception will fall quickly back into place. If you have ever exercised self-control over eating, smoking, spending, or some other behavior, you know victory comes only through endurance. We can increase our endurance by realizing that we are being molded into the likeness of Christ, the perfect image of God.

Love and affection are the roots of our efforts to change. Why should I stop my gluttonous eating and take better care of my body? Because I love God, self, and others. Why should I not carelessly waste money? Because I love and care about people who need that money. Why should I be content to live within my means? Because great happiness and peace come from accepting our boundaries and living a lower-debt, lower-stress lifestyle.

Over a two-year period I attended the Academy for Spiritual Formation, a retreat experience in a community setting offered by the Upper Room. Participants meet eight times over the two years. At the first evening worship service I attended of the Academy we said the usual words of confession, but when we silently reflected on our sin I heard one clear and unexpected word from God, "greed." I was stunned, but I also realized I was not to analyze it but to just "sit" with it. As I sat with this revelation for the week of study and reflection that followed, I realized how accurate it was. Oh, yes, I tend to be very generous with money, but my root sin might just be greed. I like being first. I like to spoil myself. I like to do what I want to do.

At heart I am very competitive. Greed has to do with excessiveness, and it is easy for a competitive person to take advantage of every opportunity that crosses her path. To do so is greedy, especially if my taking prevents someone else from receiving. At one Academy we had a massage therapist available to give ten massages. I could easily have hurried out and signed up at the top of the list, but because I was alert for greed in myself, I let others sign up. Today I am still watchful for greed in myself. I have found that if you seek solitude with God in prayer, you might just be surprised at what God says to you!

> **Reflection:** *I would invite you today to begin an examination of the deadly sins in your life. In prayerful thought, which sin is your greatest weakness? Can you see how a root sin can lead you to other sins? Write your reflection here.*

> **Prayer:** *O Jesus, help us to cut through the blinders on our spiritual eyes that prevent us from seeing the truth of our sins. Empower us to come to terms with our sins and to turn to you and repent. Amen.*

DAY TWO

THE INJUSTICE OF SIN

Scripture: This was the guilt of your sister Sodom: she and her daughters had pride, excess of food, and prosperous ease, but did not aid the poor and needy.

—*Ezekiel 16:49*

Reinhold Niebuhr wrote that the Bible defines sin in both religious and moral terms.[2] Religiously sin is rebellion against God, an attempt to take the place of God. Morally sin is injustice.

Think about gluttony for a moment. Consumption of food is a national pastime, a national disease, a national sin in our country. The person who eats excessively, to the detriment of her body, is not regarding her body as a "temple of the Holy Spirit." She is not recognizing the limits God has imposed on her body. Rather in defiance of her limitations, she continues to eat. Is this behavior sinful?

Suppose an excessive eater joins Overeaters' Anonymous or some other eating disorder group for help. Probably he does so because he is miserable and not because he thinks he is sinning against God. Our motives for change usually stem from self-centered reasons and not from believing we have sinned against God. In other words, our attitude toward sin is more self-centered than God-centered. If we diet or fight to be free of our gluttony, we do it not because gluttony is a sin against God and ourselves but because we want to fit into our clothing or we don't want to be controlled by food. We remain creatures of our culture rather than children of God, made in God's image. We have lost contact with the religious dimension of our sin.

There are also justice issues associated with gluttony. We are willing to buy the vegetables, fruits, and meats we want year-round. The agricultural industry has blossomed around the world to meet our needs because we in the West are the ones with money to pay for the produce and meat. Indigenous people in the lands where our nonseasonal foods are raised pay a very high price to satisfy our demands. Our foods are grown on the very soil that previously grew staple crops for the local people.

Here is a hypothetical case set in a single village. One family owns the largest tract of land in the village. While the family is not rich by any means, the land is rich and provides the family with sufficient food for the year, as well as enough to garner a little additional income from sales to the other villagers. The crops from the land provide one third of the village's food source as well as being a source of employment for other village members during the harvest seasons. The farm workers are thus able to purchase produce from that land. Most villagers rely on food from the large farm to supplement their own.

Enter a representative from a multinational food conglomerate. He offers this family a guaranteed contract for fifteen years to grow flowers on their land for U.S. markets. This person guarantees what seems to the family to be an enormous amount of money, regardless of what the land produces. In addition he convinces the family to buy modern farming equipment, the payments for which can be deducted from their monthly income. Using this equipment also will reduce the need for other workers on the farm. The family feels they can't pass up this opportunity, and they sign the contract.

Suddenly there is a dramatic reduction in basic foods and a corresponding increase in their price because of the scarcity. Villagers are unable to buy food from neighboring villages because their large landowners also have leased out their land to the same multinational corporation. In three years' time, malnutrition is up by 50 percent, and the infant mortality rate for children under eight has increased by 25 percent.

In a "commodity form" of economics the preeminent values are marketability and consumption. The basic problem is this: Land in developing countries is being used to produce luxury crops for supermarkets in industrialized nations, and as a result starvation and malnutrition in the developing countries are on the rise. For instance, in the 1970s in Mexico the early childhood death rate from malnutrition increased 70 percent, while the acreage of wheat, corn, beans, and rice crops declined 25 percent. In place of the basic crops strawberries and other fruits and vegetables were grown for our markets. It is an added irony for us to know that of the fruits and vegetables raised in Latin American countries, 65 percent is dumped or used for animal feed because it does not meet the beauty standards of American consumers or because the U.S. market is oversupplied.[3]

Consider Colombia, the largest supplier of flowers to our markets. Seventy percent of the land in that country is controlled by a few rich landowners. By growing carnations for export to us, they reap 80 percent more profit per acre of land than by growing local staples like wheat or corn for local consumers. The Colombian poor are not the only ones affected. Sears and Pillsbury, two large U.S. agribusiness companies, find it more profitable to import Colombian flowers to supermarket chains and franchised flower shops than to buy from U.S. growers. Since U.S. flower growers can't compete with the inexpensive Colombian imports they are forced out of business.[4] Multiply this scenario by thousands of times and you have a glimpse into today's luxury crop global economics. It's disturbing to think that people in other countries and my own are adversely affected by supplying my needs for fresh apples and beautiful flowers to grace my table all year long.

To what do we attribute the malnutrition and increased mortality rate among children—bad luck, a natural disaster, that is, an act of God, overpopulation, or a social disaster? Is this situation just? fair? What are the causal factors in this scenario? Who could possibly do something to counter or prevent this problem in the future? At the June 1997 summit for People Centered Development, speaker David Korten shared three facts that astounded me: (1) 51 of the 100 largest economies worldwide are corporations; (2) sales of the top 200 largest corporations at that time were equal to 28 percent of the total world GDP (gross domestic product) (3) there are 477 billionaires whose combined total assets roughly equal the combined annual income of the poorest 2.8 billion people on earth. The inequities reflected in these figures are shocking and deplorable.[5]

Reflection: *As flower lovers, can we justify having flowers 365 days of the year at the expense of the indigenous people in the lands where they are grown? Do we have a covenant responsibility to our brothers and sisters in these countries? Is greed a root sin in our culture? Write your reflection here.*

Prayer: *Creator of us all, have mercy on us for our hardness of heart. Forgive us for considering our comfort more important than the basic rights of other people. Forgive us for participating in an economic system that has no soul or conscience. Help us to find ways to bring good from this evil. Amen.*

DAY THREE

PATIENCE

Scripture: This is what the Lord has commanded: "Gather as much of it as each of you needs, an omer to a person according to the number of persons, all providing for those in their own tents."

—*Exodus 16:16*

Transportation is another reality to consider when we go shopping. Five hundred million gallons of fuel are required annually to transport fruits and vegetables grown in the U.S. to their markets.[6] Much of this transportation is unnecessary and nonsensical. For instance, a trucker transports Idaho potatoes to the Midwest and then drives two hundred miles, loads potatoes, and drives back to Idaho. In Indiana, a state that grows apples, you'll find apples fresh from Washington State for sale. The bottom line is that for every two dollars invested in growing food, we pay one dollar to move it.

In addition to transportation costs incurred, long-distance travel robs food of its nutritional value. For example, in a refrigerated truck broccoli loses 19 percent of its vitamin C in just twenty-four hours.[7] If broccoli is on the road four days, it has lost 34 percent of its vitamin C value! Moving most produce across the country takes five to seven days, and the journey sometimes takes two weeks.

The glut of foods and things in our markets enables greed to grow and our exaggerated expectations to become the norm. This radical change in expectations has come about over the past twenty-five years, and driving this change is the almighty dollar. Marketing creates demand. We excessively supply the "need," and we make money. As consumers we desire more; if products are supplied, we will buy. We don't have to say no to ourselves, we don't have to wait until the right season. It is unnatural to expect the nonseasonal in all seasons, but we have come to expect it. The abnormal appears to be the normal.

I want to suggest that cultivating patience is one way for us to break free from the glut of temptations that surrounds us. Patience is a virtue gained only by experiencing the need for it.

God has a perfect plan for each person's life. Our calling, our invitation is to live our life fully as the individual God created each of us to be. If we honor the first commandment, God must be the central focus of our life, the medium through which we experience life. When we are impatient, we are not content to be where we are or perhaps who we are. We want the situation to end. Patience is the calling to live with the situation by God's grace until it passes.

Patience can be a great gift when we are recovering from the death of someone we love, but patience when we want the movie to start "now," the weekend to come "now," the grocery line to dissolve "now," is a discipline. The discipline of patience requires developing the habit of living in the present moment—the only moment we truly possess. Otherwise we miss "now" while we are wanting the future. Patience is critical to the development of simplicity.

Time is a strange construct. Our emphasis is so often on *chronos* time, the linear time of minutes, hours, days. In actuality, the critical times in our individual lives are the *kairos* moments when we experience God's fullness of time for us. We know that we are exactly where we are supposed to be when we are supposed to be there. I love the imagery of Psalm 27, which begins with "The Lord is my light and my salvation: whom shall I fear? The Lord is the stronghold of my life; of whom shall I be afraid?" The psalm ends with, "I believe that I shall see the goodness of the Lord in the land of the living. Wait for the Lord; be strong and let your heart take courage; wait for the Lord!" What beautiful imagery. What wisdom!

Kairos moments are God moments, and they can come in little ways as well as big ways. The way of patience invites us to live more by *kairos* time, knowing and expecting God to work in our lives for their fullness and the furthering of the kingdom. The invitation of patience is to trust and to wait.

Patience is a key ingredient in obedience. If we believe we are not bound within a covenant relationship among God, humanity, and the rest of creation or that we are not called to live by the love ethic of Jesus, then obedience doesn't matter. Anything we do is okay; there are no rights and wrongs, only reasons and explanations. But if we believe we are called to repentance, transformation, and obedience, then cultivating our patience will empower our obedience.

If like Jesus we desire to seek and follow God's will in the everyday events of our lives, we will have to walk the path of obedience. Adhering to a covenant-relationship understanding of life with integrity requires that we hold the vision central to our lives, for it is through this lens that God reveals the world to us. Jesus needs people willing to enter the process of spiritual formation, to be conformed into his likeness, to become his disciples to his world.

Can we make a difference as disciples in the world of oversupplied vegetables, fruits, and flowers? Yes. Couldn't we accept or impose boundaries on the vegetables and fruits we consume and be patient with the seasons of the year? Couldn't we impose a "luxury tax" on ourselves when we buy out-of-season produce from developing nations and then send that money to agencies helping indigenous people in poor countries?

Can't we encourage our local grocers to handle locally grown products and commend them when they do? Can't we talk to our family and friends and share our knowledge? Can't we seek together to make our feelings known publicly or politically when appropriate? Can't we be involved in our community's decisions and help shape its future?

Reflection: How would you feel if you suddenly had to give up your favorite out-of-season foods? Where do you need to cultivate patience today? Write your reflection here.

Prayer: O Giving God of abundance, help us to receive and not to want. Help us to be grateful and not to expect demandingly. Help us to know how richly blessed we are. Amen.

DAY FOUR

FASTING

Scripture: Is not this the fast that I choose; to loose the bonds of injustice, to undo the thongs of the yoke, to let the oppressed go free, and to break every yoke?

—Isaiah 58:6

A "theology of enough"—what does it look like? How much is enough of anything? Where can we draw boundary lines in our lives? For instance, do I have to have fresh apples, oranges, and bananas twelve months of the year? How many months are enough? Do I have to buy new things each month? How frequently do I need new clothing? How much "running around in my car" is good stewardship for one person driving in today's world?

One of the most important tools in finding out "how much is enough" in the different areas of our lives is fasting—simple abstinence from food, television, negative behaviors, telephones, unnecessary doing, spending, and so on. To fast is voluntarily to deny ourselves something we normally do, for the sake of spiritual growth. Fasting, more than any other spiritual discipline, reveals what controls us. Fasting lifts the veil of denial, and we have the opportunity to see and understand ourselves far better than before. With this knowledge comes the freedom and ability to make choices about who we will be and what we will do with our lives. Not having an understanding of how much is enough in our lives leaves us victims of our own passions, whims, and impulses. We *respond* to situations rather than using forethought.

Living out faith with integrity requires the desire to change and grow spiritually.

We must maintain commitment to the singleness of purpose of our faith. People change most often as a result of desperation; they feel they are left with no other choice. But we can choose to change from *aspiration,* from the desire to be a better person, to spread the kingdom of God. Fasting as a spiritual action must always center on God. For instance, if you are fasting from food, don't spend your lunchtime out shopping but at prayer or volunteering at a soup kitchen or shelter.

My fasting from spending money on anything other than maintenance, repairs, and consumables like food has taught me about my emotional urges to buy as opposed to actual physical need. Buying gives me, as it does millions of others, a feeling of being in control, of exercising power. "I'll take that and that and wrap it, please." We are exerting power and control. (Of course the "control" is really an "out-of-control" if we are using credit cards to live beyond our means!) The question is, is a particular purchase the best choice to make? Where are the limits and boundaries to buying?

By revealing what controls us, fasting provides powerful knowledge, which we may or may not choose to act upon. For that reason there is great value and need for fasting. For instance, we need to fast from television, people, telephones, shopping, and the media, to list a few things. Fasting is an act of faith, and when we fast in communion with God, it is also an act of prayer. Think now about how you could fast regularly in ways that would empower your growth in simplicity.

Activity: *Choose something that you do daily, such as drinking coffee or watching television, and fast from doing it for several days. At the end of each day consider how you felt about the experience. Did you find yourself thinking about what you were missing? What were your thoughts? Write some notes about what you learned from fasting.*

Prayer: *Lord Jesus, empower us to fast from the things that keep us from knowing your will for us. Help us use fasting to simplify our lives and be better able to receive your spiritual guidance. Amen.*

DAY FIVE

THE TWENTY-THIRD PSALM

Scripture: *The Lord is my shepherd, I shall not want.*

—Psalm 23:1

Easter occurred two days before the bombing of the Federal Building in Oklahoma City. At the time I was living thirty-three miles northeast of Oklahoma City and literally experienced the sound and vibration of the explosion move through my house and body. I had been fishing for thoughts on a sermon or sermon series a week or two before. The themes that had come to my mind were fear, the seven deadly sins, and the Twenty-third Psalm. When the bombing occurred I knew why fear had been on my heart and why it was the topic for the next Sunday. But the urge to preach on the other two topics remained. I realized that perhaps I was to preach on those two together, so I sat down and in a manner of minutes I had divided the Twenty-third Psalm into seven parts with each part correlated to one of the deadly sins.

The sermon series touched all of us right where we live. I had no idea that some of the sins were alive and well in my own life. I hadn't realized how much power these sins hold over people's lives. They often create deep ruts that keep people going in circles rather than transcending the difficulties of life. Our minds and spirits, empowered by God, must pull us out of these ruts, so we can see and seek a vision of ourselves living full, meaningful lives. The Twenty-third Psalm is one of the paths that can lead to such a life. Although it is the most common funeral psalm, the Twenty-third Psalm is the epitome of a psalm for living.

We live in a time saturated with the marketing messages of "need me," "buy me." In the U.S. one is entitled not only to life but to the "American Dream." If you do life "well," you can have everything you want and not have much pain. After all, life is a breeze, isn't it? Yet we are assaulted daily by television, radio, billboards, newspapers, books, traffic, and noise. We are urged to be consumers and accept the motto "New is always better *and* necessary." We are distracted from enjoying our lives and what we have by our envy and greed for what we don't have. If we have four ounces in an eight-ounce cup, the world around us screams, "It's half empty!"

On the other hand, the Twenty-third Psalm tells us not only that our cup is half full but that it is overflowing. Life is not easy. Even for the most blessed among us, life is hard and full of losses—people, positions, possessions, youthfulness, and health, to mention a few major ones. But it was never our Creator's design for us to go through life alone. Rather we are accompanied and empowered by our Loving Companion. Remember the words of the psalm:

> The Lord is my shepherd, I shall not want.
> He makes me to lie down in green pastures,
> He leads me besides still waters,
> He restores my soul.
> He guides my feet in paths of righteousness for his name's sake.
> And though I walk through the valley of the shadow of death,
> I will fear no evil. For he is with me.
> His rod and his staff, they comfort me.
> He prepares a table for me in the presence of our enemies,
> He anoints my head with oil, my cup overflows
> Surely his goodness and mercy shall follow me
> All the days of my life, and I will dwell in his house forever. (AP)

Reflection: Read Psalm 23 and sit quietly in the presence of the Spirit of Life. As you read the following prayer reflection, let the Holy Spirit speak to you.

Greed. Each day we are encouraged to want more. But as sheep of the Good Shepherd we do not want; we do not lack for the essentials of life.

Think about the restfulness, the simplicity, the serenity of lying down in green pastures. The essentials of life come without threat from calm waters.

When life bumps us around and we take refuge in solitude with the Shepherd, our souls are restored.

We will do right things and be in Jesus' likeness because he will lead us for his name's sake.

We do not have to live by fear or be driven by fear. Even if we walk in the shadow of death God is with us—the all-loving, almighty One—and the signs of God's presence in our circumstances comfort us. We know God is close.

In such a situation, who needs excessive possessions and experiences—greed? Who needs to desire what someone else has—envy? Who needs to feel angry at being slighted?

As the psalmist says, "He brought me out into a broad place; he delivered me, because he delighted in me" (Psalm 18:19). Or from Psalm 66, "We went through fire and through water; yet you have brought us out to a spacious place" (Psalm 66:12).

The Shepherd provides what is needed even in the presence of enemies—envy, greed, sloth, anger, gluttony, pride, lust. Even in their midst we are anointed, consecrated, and set apart so that the oil anointing our head overflows abundantly. Can we doubt that God's blessing—God's goodness and mercy—shall follow us always and that we shall dwell in the house of the Lord forever!

Consider the following lists. Which characteristics do you prefer?

Consumption-based Life	Shepherd-led Life
Empty, wanting	Full
Slowly dying, numb	Alive
Unhappy, discontent	Content
Imprisoned by things	Free
Prisoner of desires	Satisfied
Indebted	Giving

In order to remember the knowledge we gain from living, we must put forth a significant effort. Reencountering this psalm can remind us to relax and trust. Immersing ourselves in Psalm 23 can bring a reremembrance of truth. The self-discipline to turn regularly to the scriptures and to seek solitude for listening to God undergirds our spiritual growth.

Prayer: *Great Shepherd, help us to hear your voice and choose to walk in your ways. Amen.*

ENOUGH IS ENOUGH

Opening Prayer

Giving God, you have made us for yourself. Yet in our hardheadedness, we have preferred our own lost ways to your companionship. Forgive us our sins. Forgive us for having hearts that turn inward. You are the one who made us, and you know us better than we know ourselves. Help us to hear your words of forgiveness and love. Help us to hear your invitation to come and follow you. Turn our hearts toward you and others for your glory and honor. Amen.

Discussion (Allow forty minutes.)

Let group members make notes of comments or questions about this week's material. If these issues are not touched on in the session, substitute questions generated by the group as you wish. Break into groups of three or four and discuss the following:

1. What is your understanding of the meaning of sin?
2. Examine the Ten Commandments either from Exodus 20 or Deuteronomy 5. How do the commandments form divine-human boundaries? Social boundaries?
3. Where are the boundary lines in Jesus' commandment to love our neighbor as ourselves? Jesus clarified the command by calling his disciples to love as he has loved them (John 13:34).

Essentials Exercise (Allow twenty minutes.)

Divide into pairs. Make a list of essential expenses in your lives, all the things that you need to spend money on. Read the following information about John Wesley.

A remarkable example of someone's living a "theology of enough" daily is John Wesley, the founder of Methodism. When Wesley was young, he calculated that he needed twenty-eight pounds a year to live (about $65). Since inflation was basically unknown then, he kept his level of expenditures at the same twenty-eight pounds a year for the rest of his life. Wesley's income, however, changed dramatically—from 30 pounds a year to up to 1400 pounds a year![8] The 1,372 pounds extra he gave away! What an incredible example of faith applied to one's economic life!

Could you use this example in your life? Taking into consideration inflation and future needs (like major house maintenance and replacement of appliances), in what ways could you roughly budget your future expenses and plan to give more generously to the needs of others?

Closing
Consumers' Prayer
by Joyce M. Shutt[9]

throwaway bottles
throwaway cans
throwaway friendships
throwaway fans

disposable diapers
disposable plates
disposable people
disposable wastes

instant puddings
instant rice

instant intimacy
instant ice

plastic dishes
plastic laces
plastic flowers
plastic faces

Lord of the living
transcending our lies
infuse us with meaning
recycle our lives

WEEK SIX

READ THE FOLLOWING SCRIPTURE
PASSAGE EACH DAY THIS WEEK.

The kingdom of heaven is like a mustard seed that someone took and sowed in his field; it is the smallest of all the seeds, but when it has grown it is the greatest of shrubs and becomes a tree, so that the birds of the air come and make nests in its branches.

—Matthew 13:31-32

DAY ONE

LISTENING TO THE MUSIC

Scripture: *Be still, and know that I am God!*

—Psalm 46:10

So often people think of prayer only as words we speak to God—words we read, formally recite, or speak extemporaneously to God. The Lord's Prayer and grace before meals are among the most common prayers in the lives of many Christians. The Apostle Paul admonishes us to "rejoice always, pray without ceasing, give thanks in all circumstances; for this is the will of God in Jesus Christ for you" (1 Thessalonians 5:16-17). If praying without ceasing requires constant verbal communication with God, we will be exhausted in attempting such a barrage of words! To pray means a great deal more than words. Prayer is a work of grace that is central to active faith. It is a discipline that expands our knowledge of God, the world, and ourselves. At the same time prayer transforms our circumstances and us.

Prayer, like *faith,* is an umbrella term. By this I mean the word encompasses a variety of meanings and activities and is not restricted to the limited definition of speech. We are multifaceted beings, and we pray in multifaceted ways. On the most basic level, prayer is our attitude directed toward God or awareness of God; it is an attitude of attentiveness to God. When we are attentive to God, we are also attentive to life and to ourselves; we find God in each situation because we are on the lookout for God.

Prayer is our conversation or communication with God, which may involve words, music, singing, dancing, drawing, painting, writing, studying, gardening, reflecting, silence, stillness, wonder, awe, thanksgiving, imagining, feeling, caring, loving. Other people or concerns can be at the heart of our prayer to God, whether in an act of caring or loving or in a petition of intercession on their behalf. Since prayer is a conversation or dialogue, we hear from God in scripture, books, worship, history, hymns, sermons, nature, circumstances, silence, inner assurance, peace, joy, images, dreams, the actions and presence of others, visions, the presence of the Holy Spirit within us and others, and love.

Two paths of prayer are particularly critical for transformation—solitude and silent prayer. Solitude involves drawing apart to a private, secluded place in order to be attentive to God and ourselves. While the word *solitude* implies aloneness, we can enter solitude with other people. Times of solitude and silence are common in retreats. The key is that we have drawn aside from ordinary life and experience in order to pursue silence together. An excellent group opportunity for solitude is a day retreat on a significant day, such as Good Friday, or for consideration of an important topic, such as discerning a church's mission in the community. At designated times you may break the silence and share what you are experiencing with one another.

Solitude provides the space for us to pray, to see and hear God, and to know ourselves better. To reach a place of solitude where we are free to reflect or pray upon the important things in life, we have to be silent, open, and listening. When I say silent, I mean that we have to "still the noise" that normally surrounds our lives—noise from cell phones and telephones, televisions and movies, busy streets and mechanical devices, family members and coworkers. We want to silence the world around us so that we are able to be in it—aware, alive, reflective—while not of the world, drowned out by all of its noise and words. We want to be connected to life in a very spiritual and intentional way. Our desire in seeking solitude is to be attentive to God. Solitude requires a change in our normal habits and habitats.

When we reach a place of solitude, having silenced the noisy world around us, we are free to focus our attention toward God and life. Our openness allows us to see and hear God by a thought, idea, or impression. What we experience in solitude may spark hope or give us an insight. If we pause to listen, we will find what we need. We may listen to our own hearts and minds or to nature, our environment, books, music, art, or even audiotapes.

A good biblical image of solitude is found in Elijah's encounter with God on Mount Horeb. Elijah is in flight from Jezebel after defeating the false prophets of Baal. He fasts forty days and nights as he travels to the mount of God. There he stays in a cave. God instructs him to go out and stand on the mountain before the Lord as the Lord passes. A great wind comes, as well as an earthquake and a fire, but the Lord is not in any of these. Then Elijah hears the sound of sheer silence and recognizes the Lord's presence (1 Kings 19:8-13). When we are not distracted God can get our attention. Then we can hear. In solitude we seek the place, silence, and openness in which God can speak to us. We live out Jesus' teaching "those who have ears listen."

The second path to transformation is practicing silent prayer. By silent prayer I mean unspoken prayer. (Soft meditative music and the sounds of nature can enhance silent prayer.) Practicing silent prayer is fundamental to maturing and growing in our Christian faith. There are three generally accepted forms of silent prayer—meditation, contemplation, and centering.

Meditation involves using our God-given mind to learn about God. We can meditate on many subjects—from the natural world around us to the daily paper to a conversation we had with someone. But the primary sourcebook for Christian meditation is the Bible. In meditation we use our mind to question, reason, and understand what God is revealing. For instance, we might read the story of the rich young ruler. Afterward we could ask a dozen questions, such as, Who hears this exchange between Jesus and the young man? What is at the heart of the young man's question? Is he looking for an easy way to eternal life? How would Jesus have me understand his words today?

While meditation is a highly intellectual form of prayer and seeking, it also has a loving, attentive side. In meditation we are drawn to God in love, and we seek to know what God values and how God desires to relate to us. For instance, we cannot learn about God's relationship to the poor throughout history as reflected in the Bible without meditating on the scriptures. A meditative self-examination in the light of scripture will reveal to us how far we are willing to follow where Jesus would lead. Meditation is an important form of prayer throughout our Christian life.

While meditation uses the intellectual capacities God has given us, *contemplation* engages other parts of our mind and being, so that we *experience* what is happening in a scripture passage. In contemplation we use our imaginative capacities to enter into the world of the scripture we are reading. So again if we read the story of the rich young ruler, we would let our imagination, feelings, and emotions be available to the Holy Spirit to let us experience the story. Who are we in the story? How do we feel for the poor rich man? How does Jesus show his sadness? How does the crowd feel about the exchange?

In both meditation and contemplation we are not just reliving the past but also encountering the living Lord. Both forms of prayer enrich our knowledge and experience of God and our relationship with God.

The third form of prayer is *centering prayer.* It is the most helpful in our transformation or sanctification. In centering prayer we place ourselves into the presence of God and seek to be receptive, listening to anything God might speak to us or being aware of any way God might touch us. Centering prayer requires sitting quietly before the Lord and waiting.

Centering prayer acknowledges the mystery of the indwelling Holy Spirit. Centering prayer has a significant effect on our *will* because each time we sit silently for the touch of God we are in essence surrendering ourselves to God. Our willingness allows the Spirit to touch us deeply within. In such willingness and surrender, powerful transformations take place in our lives. Our faith grows and deepens, old wounds are healed, and we come to understand ourselves much better.

Centering also releases the mind from specific thoughts. As you prepare for centering prayer and distracting thoughts enter your mind, release them as you would let balloons float away in the sky. Thoughts about what you are going to have for lunch, what so-and-so meant by a comment, whether your car really needs an oil change—all these thoughts you let go. This process is like trying to become the eye of the hurricane, stillness in the midst of a noisy mind. To help with this process, identify a short word to say that recenters you and releases these stray thoughts. When your mind wanders off (as it usually will!), gently recall yourself to silence by saying your word silently in your mind. Feel the meaning of the word come alive in you. My word is *shalom*. When I say it in my mind, I think of peace and release all the thoughts bombarding me.

I find metaphors and images helpful ways to understand mysteries. Dance is a beautiful image for what we seek to do with God in solitude and prayer. When both dancers try to lead, the dance is awkward and jerky, but when a masterful dancer leads and the partner follows, the dance is smooth and beautiful. In solitude and prayer we dance with God. A simple way to empower this image is to reflect on the word *guidance*. If we split up the word g-u-i-dance we can see: "God you and I dance!" Remembering this helps me to listen for the music, relax, and let God lead.

I encourage you to broaden your prayer experience and make the commitment to set aside regular time for dancing with God.

> **Reflection:** *Find a place of solitude today. Try to spend at least ten minutes engaged in meditation, contemplation, or centering prayer. Afterward write your reflection here.*

> **Prayer:** *Help us to be silent so that we can hear you, Holy One. Give us spiritual ears to hear and eyes to see. Amen.*

DAY TWO

CONTINUAL RENEWAL

Scripture: *Do not be conformed to this world, but be transformed by the renewing of your minds, so that you may discern what is the will of God—what is good and acceptable and perfect.*

—Romans 12:2

Growth in the spiritual life has to be intentional. If we aim at nothing, we will surely hit it. While we Christians are not all in agreement about whether women can be ministers, whether sprinkling really counts for baptism, or whether Jesus accepted homosexuals, we do recognize Jesus' calling to all who would be disciples is simply, "Deny yourself, pick up your cross and follow me."

While in my first full-time pastorate, I came to the realization that Jesus' main point was not about my picking up my personal cross and bearing it (each person has his or her own cross). Rather Jesus is calling his disciples to pick up our part of *his cross*—a cross of righteousness, compassion, and justice. He is asking us to give up some of our comfort and ease so that others can live more fully. He is asking us to live meaningful lives.

In reality the cross is a double-sided gift. It is a gift to be freed from conformity to this world. It is a gift to be able to treasure spiritual truths above earthen pleasures. The cross we bear is one of deep joy because when we carry it we live in shalom, at least part of the time.

The task we are called to is formidable! But the Caller supplies the grace we need. We can plug into this power by heeding Paul's advice found in Romans 12:2: "Do not be conformed to this world, but be transformed by the renewing of your minds, so that you may discern what is the will of God." To recognize and act on what we understand God's will to be in specific circumstances empowers us to make wise choices and to be in right standing with God. As people called to be in Christ's likeness of righteousness, compassion, and justice, we are to look not at our own interests but at the interests of others with the mind of Christ (Philippians 2:4-5). To put on the mind of Christ we must be transformed for the sake of discernment. The mind must constantly be in the process of renewal, refreshment, and relearning.

There are at least two significant ways to renew our mind. The first is to guide our mind by prayer and reading. The second is to control our feelings that may overwhelm us. The battle of faith is fought in our mind. What we think will determine who we are. If we think we can do something, we probably will. If our mind only takes in what our environment feeds it, we are in serious trouble! Remember the workings of the addictive system. The cultural mindset says: "Think first about you." "You need this car." "You are incomplete without this house." "You're too old to change." "You need to upgrade." Life is not easy and faith is not simple. We have to be strong to live by a value system different from the status quo.

There are dozens of ways to guide what we think and believe by prayer and reading. Prayer in a broad sense speaks of our attentiveness to God. To put on a prayerful attitude is to see life through the eyes of our body, soul, and spirit. We see the higher values at play and are able to live in each moment.

What we choose to read is of the greatest importance. Read a wide range of materials—Scripture, old classics, devotional books, great literature. The actual act of reading may be done alone, in a group, with a friend, or by listening to tapes. Having one friend with whom to study and think out loud can make a tremendous difference in our world. There is strength in numbers, especially when we are going against the tide!

Scripture gives us guidance about what should occupy our mind: "Finally, beloved, whatever is true, whatever is honorable, whatever is just, whatever is pure, whatever is pleasing, whatever is commendable, if there is any excellence and if there is anything worthy of praise, think about these things" (Philippians 4:8). Does that mean we can't think about bridge or read our favorite fiction writer? Absolutely not. It does mean we need to think about positive, life-affirming matters—about matters that make a difference for other people as well as ourselves.

Regular doses of uplifting and inspiring readings encourage us all. The *Chicken Soup for the Soul* books have exploded in popularity because they give us positive story after positive story of people overcoming difficulties. We need healthful food to overcome the flood of negative messages we receive daily from the world around us. We will have to tend our mind well to live in ways that make a positive difference to the people around us.

Secondly, we need to control feelings and desires that may overwhelm us and direct our behavior. We need to subject these feelings and desires to discernment. In other words, with our mind we assess our feelings—their rightness or appropriateness. Feelings are powerful; don't ever underestimate them. Sensing feelings can be very important in our faith journey and our relationships with others, but our mind has to be stronger than our feelings. For instance, when we really want to buy something we don't need, we can turn our mind to the power and source for resistance. We can call in the troops for help!

Living alone for many years, it was easy for me to fall into the habit of pampering myself. The way I figured it, I would be pampering someone else if a person were here, so why not pamper me? I would regularly "treat" myself to little gifts. One Saturday during my years in seminary, I had to stop by the shoe repair shop on my way out of town. The store sold beautiful handmade leatherwork. At the time I needed a notepad cover, so when I saw a fabulous piece of leather I was overcome with desire. Full of rationalizations I ordered one, leaving a $50 deposit! As I drove to my churches I kept feeling uncomfortable. What in the world had I done? What was I thinking of when I ordered a $150 elegant leather notepad on my annual salary of less than $12,000? Would such a striking pad be appropriate for a minister in my circumstances? My feelings remained disrupted, desolate. When I looked at the situation I realized that it was ludicrous for me in my economic and ministerial lifestyle to order such a gift for myself. I resolved to right the situation, and as soon as I arrived, I called and cancelled the order! The woman who owned the store was very understanding and accommodating, and I was filled with relief and joy. Because I listened and discerned my feelings, I was free to correct my earlier action based on impulsive desires.

A right feeling or desire will still be right if you take the time to discern its origin. To discern where a feeling comes from, ask yourself, Is this feeling a gift from God? Is this feeling a desire to be "in control"? Is this feeling an irresponsible urge that moves me to buy this knickknack? If a feeling can't stand the examination, you know it is not the right one to follow.

Thank goodness we are called to be faithful and not perfect! If we carefully guide our mind by prayer and reading and use our mind to control the feelings that may overwhelm us, we will be successful in "renewing our minds so that we may discern the will of God." Our renewing is continual, a lifelong process.

Reflection: Simply think on what your Creator loves most about you.

Prayer: Thank you that you do not call us to walk in a path without giving us the power to do so. Thanks be to God!

DAY THREE

MAKING A DIFFERENCE

Scripture: Strive first for the kingdom of God and his righteousness, and all these things will be given to you as well.

—Matthew 6:33

Bearing the cross of Jesus is loving others as Jesus would. His cross is made of the wood of compassion, righteousness, and justice. We will never be perfect at bearing Christ's cross, and that is all right. After all, we are only human! The most important thing is that we embrace simplicity and try, that we open ourselves to a deeper vision or value in life and strive to live out this kingdom vision with integrity.

It wouldn't be natural if we didn't raise the question, Can we really make a difference worth the effort? The story of the little girl who went walking along the beach with her grandfather tells me the answer is yes. The grandfather and the girl came upon a section of beach covered with starfish that had washed up on the shore. The little girl began to pick up starfish and throw them back into the water. Her grandfather called out to her that she couldn't possibly make a dent in the pile of starfish and to give up. She held up a single starfish and answered, "Perhaps so, Papa, but it makes a difference to this one," and she tossed it into the sea and leaned over to pick up another.

God only asks us to make a difference where we are. The way each of us expresses economic simplicity in our life will directly relate to who we are and what we do. In other words, if our simplicity is focused in God's kingdom, it will take a shape and form appropriate to us as individuals. There is not a quantifiable "standard" by which we must live.

Consider the example of two people. Person A works for UPS, has no children, and loves art. Person B owns a title company, has three children, and has a passion for music. Their wardrobes will not look remotely the same; nor will their houses. Yet both persons can reflect commitment to good economic stewardship. They can have nice clothing without having an excessive amount. They can be conservative in their use of natural resources. They can be generous with their wealth. They can both avoid buying things they don't really need or use sufficiently to justify the investment. They can both buy things jointly with others in order to share the cost and the use.

The biggest impact we can make is not through our words but through who we are and what we do. We make a difference when we are people of faith whose integrity in actions follows from who we are as people, that is, our inner being. We become at least struggling models of an active living faith.

The good news is that many people have walked the path of faith before us, as well as with us now. This true story took place in and around the Eastminster Presbyterian Church in a suburb of Wichita, Kansas.[1] The church had launched a $525,000 building program when earthquakes devastated thousands of homes and buildings in Guatemala. At a board of elders meeting, a layman asked how they could buy an ecclesiastical Cadillac when their brothers and sisters in Guatemala had just lost their Volkswagen. The elders agreed. They modified their building program, paid their architect, and settled for a $180,000 alternative. They then sent their pastor and two elders to Guatemala to find out how they could help the Christians there.

After the team reported back to the board of elders, the whole congregation enthusiastically backed the borrowing of $120,000 from a local bank to rebuild twenty-six churches and twenty-eight pastors' homes in Guatemala! Inspired by Eastminster's example, another congregation modified its building plans and sent $60,000 for aid to Guatemala. Continued inspiration led a church in India to raise $1,200 for Guatemalan relief!

What a wonderful account of churches deciding "how much is enough" and generously giving away the rest. In this case the Eastminster church still borrowed money as they had intended, but they used it for others instead of themselves.

Simplicity invites us to focus on kingdom discipleship as we pick up our cross and follow Jesus. Thank goodness we do not have to walk alone! We walk with the Holy Spirit and with one another. Thanks be to God.

> *Reflection: Take the rest of your prayer period to really think about what priority guides your life. Or in different words, around what is your life organized or disorganized? Is this the focus you want for your life? Write your reflection here.*

> *Prayer: Transforming Spirit, come renew us this day. Give us vision to see the truth, and give us power to adhere to the truth. Amen and amen.*

DAY FOUR

REDIRECTION

Scripture: *I can do all things through him who strengthens me.*

—Philippians 4:13

FACT: There are more children living in poverty today than there were 10 years ago.[2]

FACT: In the year 2000, the world's daily currency markets exchange is $1.5 trillion, yet more than 1.2 billion people live on less than $1 a day.[3]

FACT: Multinational corporations use advertising campaigns to communicate to poverty-stricken worlds what the affluent life is like, convincing the poor to spend their money on unnecessary products like tobacco and soft drinks. For instance, at one time the Nestlé Corporation passed out free samples of infant formula while recommending to women in developing nations that they use it rather than nurse their children.[4] The use of formula resulted in mothers' being unable to produce milk and hence being forced to buy formula in packages that they often were unable to read. These women often lacked access to sanitary water for mixing the formula. This circumstance combined with the lack of immunological protection found in breast milk resulted in severe malnutrition and diarrhea in infants. Bottle-fed babies are as much as twenty-five times more likely to die than infants exclusively breast-fed for the first six months of life.[5]

The battle for more money leaves a trail of broken lives. Life is not fair. But no matter where you look, the happiest people are those who are grateful. Somehow gratitude seems to go hand-in-hand with contentedness. Paul claims this gift when he writes to the Philippians:

Not that I am referring to being in need; for I have learned to be content with whatever I have. I know what it is to have little, and I know what it is to have plenty. In any and all circumstances I have learned the secret of being well-fed and of going hungry, of having plenty and of being in need. I can do all things through him who strengthens me. (Philippians 4:11-13)

If we see God radically active in our life, then we realize that God's provision will always be enough. The Spirit gives us the strength for gratitude in times of abundance and in times of want. If I were going to reduce this truth to a formula it would be:

Realization of the blessing we possess

+ assessment of how much is enough (i.e., how much we *need* to live)

= empowerment to reduce what we *want*.

This empowerment also encourages us to redirect part of our blessing on behalf of God and others.

Below is a list of some of the practical ways that keep me focused on my faith as I seek to live a more responsible and faithful economic life. Try them for yourself.

- Seek pleasure in what you don't have to own by appreciating the world around you. Find places of physical beauty and enjoy the special gifts of nature or enterprise. Go exploring or walking. Read a book or just sit and be. Have a picnic or go to a museum. Sit in a favorite café and dine with a friend.
- Practice detachment from things. Periodically or when the opportunity arises, give away things you value to others who can use them or will appreciate them. It is very liberating.
- Be aware of how much of everything you use. For instance, you could be aware this month of your water consumption. When you have a portion of a glass of water left, do you toss it in the sink or pour it on a plant or in your pet's water bowl? Do you run the water when you brush your teeth? Conservation is smart.

- Charge yourself a "luxury tax" on out-of-season fruits, vegetables, and flowers that you buy. Also charge a tax when you use an excessive amount of any primary resource like water or gasoline. Give the "tax" money you have set aside to a charity that works on behalf of the poor.
- Remember and practice the Four Rs—Reduce, Reuse, Recycle, and Redistribute.
- Regularly fast from food or television for the purpose of spending the time in prayer or reading. Observe Lent each year as a special time of fasting.
- Don't buy anything "just" because it is on sale, especially if you are going into debt to do so. Calculate discount versus genuine need.
- Don't buy on the basis of feelings. Subject feelings to discernment. Ask, Is this what I'm supposed to buy with this money? Is this a wise investment?
- Be an accountable steward of all your economic resources.
- Be conservative across the board in consumption.
- Be open to short- or long-term vows related to economic simplicity. If your weight is stable, you might vow not to buy new clothes for a year. If you already have lots of books to read, you might not buy any books for a year. Concentrate on reading those you have or visit your community library.
- Be grateful for all you have. Cultivate an attitude of gratitude.
- Be alert to the marketing efforts you encounter. Many outlandish claims are made through the lens of sex. What a sexy woman should have to do with the water you drink, I haven't the foggiest notion. What matters is the purity of the water, not that a gorgeous woman walking on a beach drinks it. The type of jeans you wear will not determine the success of your intimacy with another. Help children and others see the absurdity and addiction in the superficial life portrayed in such marketing efforts.
- Resist driving short distances. Either walk or bike. If you are unsure whether a store carries what you want, call before making an unnecessary trip.
- Study the topic of simplicity further. An annotated list of resources in this book will guide you to some useful books.

- Send monetary gifts to people you know are struggling financially—perhaps a divorced friend with children, a widow on a small pension, or a college student. It is a wonderful gift to be able to help others.
- Buy locally and encourage merchants to carry local products—from grocery produce to art.
- If you are part of an investment plan, encourage the company to invest in life-affirming stocks, bonds, and other investment vehicles. There are some wonderful investments that offer small loans to poor people in depressed economies. It doesn't matter if the return is less, although I'm not saying it would be. The primary issue is one of value. Helping others is more important than making money. God is more important than mammon.
- When all else fails, go outside when there is a breeze and feel the wind on your face—the wind you cannot see—and reremember the miracle of life around you.

In summary, live with the awareness that there is a cost for the luxury we live in. Treasure and respect that cost and try to make some compensations for the unfairness of the situation. Life will be unfair, but we can make it more just.

Reflection: Think about how you could use "luxury taxes" you impose on yourself. Who might be good recipients? Write your reflection here.

Prayer: Thank goodness you are able, Lord, to lead us into faithful paths. Amen.

DAY FIVE

LOVING

Scripture: *God is love, and those who abide in love abide in God, and God abides in them.*

—1 John 4:16

A patient in the hospice where I work asked me to state simply what I believe living is all about. After a moment's pause, my response was "to love and be loved." I had never reduced life to five little words before. I had to stop and think if this was what I really thought. My conclusion was and is yes.

I strongly believe our loving involves not just other people but all of creation. We love God directly in our hearts and through loving life—people, nature, and ourselves. There are many paths to God, and we need to use as many of them as we can. Visualize a wheel on which God is at the center and we are the outer rim. Each spoke is a path to God. The more spokes we have, the more in touch we are with the creative, sustaining Force of life.

"To love and be loved" covers all the fronts. The more important of the two halves is "to love." To love requires a certain detachment from our own ego. We have to be free or empty of ourselves enough to make space for others in our heart. In loving, our heart turns outward toward others.

On the other hand, to "be loved" is a blessed state of affairs too! Nothing makes a flower bloom more than the sun. So it is with people who are loved. Accepting and experiencing being loved is the most powerful force in the universe. While "to love" is the more important gift to strive toward, the power to step out in love requires our first realizing we are loved by God. We have to feel that life is for us and not against us.

Love is a circle—the more you give out the more it comes back to you. Loving others brings love into our lives. Similarly, caring for others in a multitude of ways brings meaning to our existence. My deepest prayer is to be a vessel of God for others, which is why I treasure this prayer by Saint Francis of Assisi.[6]

> Lord, make me an instrument of thy peace;
> Where there is hatred, let me sow love;
> where there is injury, pardon;
> where there is doubt, faith;
> where there is despair, hope;
> where there is darkness, light;
> and where there is sadness, joy.
> O divine Master,
> Grant that I not so much seek to be consoled as to console;
> to be understood, as to understand;
> to be loved, as to love;
> for it is in giving that we receive,
> it is in pardoning that we are pardoned,
> And it is in dying that we are born to eternal life.

God is the source of healing and hope. How awesome it is to spread both by loving. John of the epistles helps us understand what this loving and being loved is all about. In the First Letter of John he writes, "God is love, and those who abide in love abide in God, and God abides in them" (1 John 4:16). If the first commandment is to love God with our whole being, then we are invited to love, to dwell in the greatest positive force in nature, love. Moreover, we can see God's love in one another. John writes, "No one has ever seen God; if we love one another, God lives in us" (1 John 4:12). If we love God, we will love those whom God treasures. We will be concerned for the needs of others, be they physical, emotional, relational, spiritual, or economic. John wants us to understand that loving other people and loving God are the same kind of love.

Loving is a demanding task. I imagine most of you know that. It requires openness, patience, and respect. When we are prayerful, we are open. Think of prayer as attentiveness to God and to your life. Be open to promptings regarding other people, even strangers—to call, write, give a gift, answer a question, and so forth. Secondly, to be loving we have to be patient—willing to wait on God and others as we work within the situation where we find ourselves.

Lastly, to respect one another is at the heart of loving. My dad taught me about respect not only by the way he always treats people but also by a particularly memorable lesson when I was sixteen years old. We were at our local full-service gas station. When the attendant brought me the charge slip to sign, I never looked up at him. Then I started the car in the midst of our transaction. As I drove off my dad strongly reprimanded me and said not to treat anyone so thoughtlessly again. I should acknowledge the person and look at him. In my heart I knew my dad was right. I have since tried always to be attentive to people and not be rude and discourteous.

John goes on to write that the one in us is greater than the one who is in the world (1 John 4:4). That's a relief! So "let us love, not in word or speech, but in truth and action" (1 John 3:18). Let our lives reveal our faith. For "whatever is born of God conquers the world. And this is the victory that conquers the world, our faith" (1 John 5:4). This is a full-scale pep talk to boost our perseverance in the life of faith. God will be faithful in giving us the strength we need to love others and to accept their love.

My international friends at seminary taught me many lessons in economics and in love. In my typical U.S.A. way, I wanted to take two special friends, Thelma and Glenna, on a small buying spree for their Christmas presents. As providence would have it, my car was struck in a hit-and-run accident the weekend before we were to go. Both women adamantly refused shopping and insisted on redirecting that money to the deductible on my car repair. I was embarrassed to compare our values. I wanted to give them an American shopping spree, and they wanted to spend the money in a more practical way by fixing my car. Their gift and their wisdom blessed me.

Reflection: *What people in your life have mirrored God's love for you? Reflect on memories of these persons and their actions. Write your reflection here.*

Prayer: *Love is the answer and the way. Gentle One, help us to be great lovers. Amen.*

GROUP SESSION

A TIME TO CHOOSE

Note: This closing session will run a little over one hour.

Opening Prayer

Thank you, Creating One, for bringing us to this place and to the beginning of the rest of our lives. Be with us in the stewardship of this marvelous gift of life that you have given us. Help us to accept you as a companion and to receive those whom you send to journey with us. May you be praised by the way we live our lives. Amen.

Reading (Allow five to eight minutes for everyone to read these concluding comments to the six-week study.)

For a Christian, an economic system is a means to an end—a mechanism for exchanging goods and services. The economic system in which we live is a reality of everyday life, nothing more. We steer our lives by a higher value—the love ethic of Jesus. Central to our bearing the cross is our acceptance of Jesus' love and our attentiveness to the needs of others. Love, not mammon, must be our guiding light.

Each of us can choose to change out of aspiration rather than desperation. We have the choice to live our faith. But living our faith will require "righteousness," that is, a genuine relationship with God. Compassion will be our guiding light, our rule in life. Justice will lead us to faithful stewardship—to care for and work on behalf of others in the global community. Shalom will be our reward.

Matthew beautifully expresses Jesus' calling:

> Let me tell you why you are here. You're here to be salt-seasoning that brings out the God-flavors of this earth. If you lose your saltiness, how will

people taste godliness? You've lost your usefulness and will end up in the garbage.

Here's another way to put it: You're here to be light, bringing out the God-colors in the world. God is not a secret to be kept. We're going public with this, as public as a city on a hill. If I make you light-bearers, you don't think I'm going to hide you under a bucket, do you? I'm putting you on a light stand. Now that I've put you there on a hilltop, on a light stand–shine! Keep open house; be generous with your lives. By opening up to others, you'll prompt people to open up with God, this generous Father in heaven. (Matthew 5:13-16, MESSAGE)

Jesus' presence in the life of Zacchaeus certainly made a shining lamp and a strong salt out of Zacchaeus. Now it is our turn, our time to get out on a limb of prayer, a limb of silence, a limb of action. Now is the time to learn what it means to be renewed.

May God richly bless you!

Discussion (Allow about thirty-five minutes.)

Since this is your last session together in this study, do what works the best for your group. Here are three questions that could be discussed in small groups. If other issues have been raised in your group and you want to spend this session exploring those, do so. Return to the large group for sharing and group closure.

1. What ideas spoke to you most in this study?
2. In what arenas of your life do you feel challenged to grow? Do you want to grow in this area(s)?
3. Pick an area for growth and give one another suggestions to help form a plan for growth.

Closing Service (Allow thirty minutes.)

Before beginning the service, look over it and assign parts. Be as creative as you can. For instance, for the invocation ask different people to read each stanza, then have all read the last stanza together.

SILENCE Sit in silence for three to five minutes.

INVOCATION
Consumers' Prayer
by Joyce M. Shutt[7]

throwaway bottles
throwaway cans
throwaway friendships
throwaway fans

disposable diapers
disposable plates
disposable people
disposable wastes

instant puddings
instant rice
instant intimacy
instant ice

plastic dishes
plastic laces
plastic flowers
plastic faces

Lord of the living
transcending our lies
infuse us with meaning
recycle our lives

PRAYER OF CONFESSION

Lord, we confess our day to day failure to be truly human.

Lord, we confess to you.

Lord, we confess that we often fail to love with all we have and are, often because we do not fully understand what loving means, often because we are afraid of risking ourselves.

Lord, we confess to you.

Lord, we cut ourselves off from each other and we erect barriers of division.

Lord, we confess to you.

Lord, we confess that by silence and ill-considered word

we have built up walls of prejudice.

Lord, we confess that by selfishness and lack of sympathy

we have stifled generosity and left little time for others.

Holy Spirit, speak to us. Help us listen to your word of forgiveness, for we are very deaf. Come, fill this moment and free us from sin.[8]

Let us remember and take comfort in the knowledge that when we are faithful to confess our sins, God is faithful to forgive our sins! Alleluia! Amen!

SCRIPTURE READING

Old Testament: Micah 6:8. "He has told you, O mortal, what is good; and what does the Lord require of you but to do justice, and to love kindness, and to walk humbly with your God?"

Sharing: Share in the large group where you feel God is calling you to grow in economic simplicity.

New Testament: Luke 19:1-10. "He entered Jericho and was passing through it. A man was there named Zacchaeus; he was a chief tax collector and was rich. He was trying to see who Jesus was, but on account of the crowd he could not, because he was short in stature. So he ran ahead and climbed a sycamore tree to see him, because he was going to pass that way. When Jesus came to the place, he looked up and said to him, 'Zacchaeus, hurry and come down; for I must stay at your house today.' So he hurried down and was happy to welcome him. All who saw it began to grumble and said, 'He has gone to be the guest of one who is a sinner.' Zacchaeus stood there and said to the Lord, 'Look, half of my possessions, Lord, I will give to the poor; and if I have defrauded anyone of anything, I will pay back four times as much.' Then Jesus said to him, 'Today salvation has come to this house, because he too is a son of Abraham. For the Son of Man came to seek out and to save the lost.'"

Sharing: Share with the person next to you how Zacchaeus's story touches you. Does God speak to you at any point in this story?

PRAYERS OF INTERCESSION

Let people spontaneously lift up concerns on behalf of the world. After each, respond with, "Loving One, hear our prayer." Use the prayer time to call upon the Lord to act on our behalf.

CLOSING

A Meditation Based on the Beatitudes[9]

People who do not hold tightly to things are happy,
  because all of God's kingdom is theirs.
People who are gentle with the earth
  will see it blossom forever.
People who can cry for all the world's suffering,
  will live to see happiness.
People who hunger and thirst for what is right,
  will finally have their fill.

People who really care,

will find love wherever they go.

People who don't let the world get them down,

will see God.

People who make peace happen,

are God's children.

People who give up their own comfort so that others can be helped,

know what heaven is all about.

LORD, LET US BE LIKE THESE!

SENDING FORTH

LEADER: Go forth with God's help and be the best you that you can be! Blessings of shalom on each of you.

ALL: We go forth with God's help. We treasure the gift of life and give thanks for it, as we seek to be molded into the likeness of Christ for the sake of the world around us. Peace be with us. Amen and amen.

NOTES

WEEK ONE

1. Howard A. Snyder, *EarthCurrents* (Nashville, Tenn.: Abingdon Press, 1995), 13.

2. J. Richard Peck, "The Trial of Adam and Eve," *Circuit Rider* (May 1994):3.

3. Anne Wilson Schaef, *When Society Becomes an Addict* (San Francisco: Harper & Row, 1987), 18–19.

4. Ibid., 45.

5. Anne Wilson Schaef, *Beyond Therapy, Beyond Science* (San Francisco: Harper Collins, 1992), 208.

6. Richard J. Foster, *Freedom of Simplicity* (San Francisco: Harper & Row, 1981), 3.

7. E. F. Schumacher, *Small Is Beautiful* (New York: Harper & Row, 1973), 48.

8. John Kavanaugh as quoted in Marilyn Helmuth Voran, *Add Justice to Your Shopping List* (Scottdale, Pa.: Herald Press 1986), 7.

9. Laura Meagher, *Teaching Children about Global Awareness* (New York: Crossroad, 1991), 86–87.

10. Laurence Shames, *The Hunger for More* (New York: Vintage Books, 1989), 29.

11. Ibid., 30–31.

12. *The United Methodist Hymnal* (Nashville, Tenn.: The United Methodist Publishing House, 1989), 893.

WEEK THREE

1. Thomas H. Green, *When the Well Runs Dry* (Notre Dame, Ind.: Ave Maria Press, 1979), 143.

2. Alan Richardson, ed., *A Theological Word Book of the Bible* (New York: Macmillan Publishing Company, 1950), 75.

3. Richard J. Foster, *The Challenge of the Disciplined Life* (San Francisco: Harper & Row, 1985), 71-73.

4. Kenneth E. Boulding, "The Economics of the Coming Spaceship Earth," in *Economics, Ecology, Ethics,* ed. Herman E. Daly (San Francisco: W.H. Freeman and Company, 1980), 258.

NOTES

WEEK FOUR

1. From *The Empty Place* (Franciscan Communication Center, 1976) as cited in *Experiencing More with Less* by Meredith Sommers Dregni (Scottdale, Pa.: Herald Press, 1983), 100.

WEEK FIVE

1. William R. White, *Fatal Attractions* (Nashville, Tenn.: Abingdon Press, 1992), 11–12.
2. Reinhold Niebuhr, *Human Nature,* vol. 1 of *The Nature and Destiny of Man* (New York: Charles Scribner's Sons, 1964), 179.
3. Voran, *Add Justice to Your Shopping List,* 22.
4. Ibid, 21.
5. David C. Korten, presentation at plenary session of the Peoples' Summit 1997, Denver, Colorado, June 20, 1997 at http://iisd1.iisd.ca/pcdf/archives.htm#1997.
6. Voran, *Add Justice to Your Shopping List,* 24–25.
7. Ibid., 25.
8. Foster, *Freedom of Simplicity,* 131.
9. Joyce M. Shutt, "Consumers' Prayer," *Living More with Less* by Doris Janzen Longacre (Scottdale, Pa.: Herald Press, 1980), 14.

WEEK SIX

1. Longacre, *Living More with Less,* 235–36.
2. *The State of the World's Children 2000* (New York: UNICEF), 51.
3. Ibid., 22.
4. Danny Duncan Collum, "Nestlé Boycott: The Sequel," *Sojourners* (October 1989): 8.
5. *The State of the World's Children 1990* (Oxford: Oxford University Press), 26.
6. *The United Methodist Hymnal* (Nashville, Tenn.: The United Methodist Publishing House, 1989), 481.
7. Cited in Longacre, *Living More with Less,* 14.
8. *The United Methodist Hymnal,* 893.
9. Cited in Dregni, *Experiencing More with Less,* 100.

RESOURCES

Allen, Joseph L. *Love and Conflict.* Lanham, Md.: University Press of America, 1995.

Bellah, Robert N. et al. *The Good Society.* New York: Vintage Books, 1991.

Birch, Bruce C. *What Does The Lord Require? The Old Testament Call to Social Witness.* Philadelphia, Pa.: The Westminster Press, 1985. Examines how the Old Testament traditions should influence the contemporary Christian church's social witness. Discusses the ethics of being as well as the ethics of doing.

Collum, Danny Duncan. "Nestlé Boycott: The Sequel," *Sojourners* (October 1989): 8.

Cooper, David A. *Silence, Simplicity, and Solitude.* Woodstock, Ver.: SkyLight Paths Publishing, 1999. Excellent resource for planning spiritual retreats—times of solitude with God. According to the author, the biggest demon we face is our sense of lost time. The book examines different traditions of spiritual practice and outlines how to set up a retreat. Even if one is doing only a three-hour retreat at home, there are good ideas to recreate in your own circumstances.

Corson, J. Kenneth. *Lifestyle: Reflection on Faith.* Lineville, Ala.: SIFAT, 1991. A wonderfully powerful short book that unites Christian faith belief and lifestyle as one. *Lifestyle* challenges you to really examine your faith.

DeWaal, Esther. *The Way of Simplicity.* Maryknoll, N.Y.: Orbis Books, 1998. This book presents spirituality and simplicity in the Cistercian tradition. The book's vision is to integrate our spiritual selves with our daily routine.

Diehl, William E. *The Monday Connection.* San Francisco: HarperSanFrancisco, 1991. A Christian layman takes his faith into his Monday workplace. God is in our everyday life; we just have to look. Lots of good food for thought and action.

Dorr, Donal. *Spirituality and Justice.* Maryknoll, N.Y.: Orbis Books, 1984. Using Micah 6:8 as the definitive Scripture for a balanced spirituality, Dorr calls his readers to open to conversion on moral, social, and political levels. His discussions of prayers of petition and providence are especially noteworthy.

Dregni, Meredith Sommer. *Experiencing More With Less.* Scottdale, Pa.: Herald Press, 1983.

Elgin, Duane. *Voluntary Simplicity.* New York: Harper Trade, 1998. Thought-provoking secular book that examines the world and investigates what a voluntary choice for simplicity might look like. Describes a way of life that is outwardly simple and inwardly rich.

Foster, Richard J. *Celebration of Discipline.* San Francisco: HarperSanFrancisco, 1998. Classic book on thirteen different spiritual disciplines that promote spiritual growth. Includes section on "Simplicity."

———. *The Challenge of the Disciplined Life.* San Francisco: Harper & Row, 1985. Struggles with the issues of faithful Christian living in the areas of money, sex, and power. Excellent, thought-provoking book.

———. *Freedom of Simplicity.* San Francisco: Harper & Row, 1981. Develops models for achieving simplicity based on the priority of seeking first the kingdom of God and his righteousness. The very complicated issues of living are woven with Christian disciplines such as prayer and solitude to create a fabric of economic simplicity.

Green, Thomas H. *When The Well Runs Dry.* Notre Dame, Ind.: Ave Maria Press, 1979.

Job, Rueben P. and Norman Shawchuck. *A Guide to Prayer for All God's People.* Nashville, Tenn.: Upper Room Books, 1994.

Kavanaugh, John Francis. *Following Christ in a Consumer Society.* Maryknoll, N.Y.: Orbis Books, 1981. An intense book that goes to the heart of today's consumer society, calling for Christians to recognize their values and live by them. Good analysis of our culture's moral behavior.

Kaylor, R. David. *Jesus the Prophet: His Vision of the Kingdom on Earth.* Louisville, Ky.: Westminster John Knox Press, 1994.

Keating, Thomas. *Intimacy with God.* New York: Crossroad, 1996.

Longacre, Doris Janzen. *Living More with Less.* Scottdale, Pa.: Herald Press, 1980. Commissioned by the Mennonites in response to the inequities of the world's resource distribution, they also sought to bring a Christian perspective to material consumption. It is a book about the truth of reality; it is about life standards based on commitment and value. The book is packed full of practical ideas. It is now out of print but worth looking up in a library.

May, Gerald G. *Addiction and Grace.* San Francisco: HarperSanFrancisco, 1991.

———. "Gerald May on Addiction and Prayer" *Praying* 49 (July-August 1992): 18–21.

Meagher, Laura. *Teaching Children about Global Awareness.* New York: Crossroad, 1991. Beautiful argument and material for teaching our children (and learning ourselves) about fundamental global human issues. Set within a Christian ethical context, it is an excellent resource book for ideas and facts.

Meeker-Lowry, Susan. *Economics As If the Earth Really Mattered.* North Kingston, R.I.: New Society Publishers, 1988.

Moxnes, Halvor. *The Economy of the Kingdom.* Minneapolis, Minn.: Augsburg Fortress, 1988.

Niebuhr, Reinhold. *Human Nature.* Vol. 1 of *The Nature and Destiny of Man.* New York: Charles Scribner's Sons, 1964.

Rohr, Richard. *Simplicity: The Art of Living.* New York: Crossroad, 1992.

Schaef, Anne Wilson. *When Society Becomes an Addict.* San Francisco: Harper & Row, 1987. Challenging book that analyzes contemporary society and labels its complex behavioral systems as similar to those of a drug addict. The book takes a close look at the characteristics and processes of the addictive system.

———. *Beyond Therapy, Beyond Science.* San Francisco: HarperSanFrancisco, 1992.

Schumacher, E. F. *Small Is Beautiful.* New York: Harper & Row, 1975.

Shames, Laurence. *The Hunger for More.* New York: Vintage Books, 1991.

Shue, Henry. *Basic Rights: Subsistence, Affluence, and U.S. Foreign Policy.* Princeton, N.J.: Princeton University Press, 1980.

Sider, Ronald J. *Rich Christians in an Age of Hunger.* Nashville, Tenn.: Word Publishing, 1990. In-depth and powerful look at the bibilical perspective on economics. Sider moves from the authoritative vision and challenge of Scripture to its implementation today in our daily lives.

Snyder, Howard A. *EarthCurrents.* Nashville, Tenn.: Abingdon Press, 1995. Seeing "now" as a hinge in history, this book traces and forecasts eight worldview trends from 1990–2030: (1) the online, instant-access culture, (2) the rise of a global economy, (3) the roles and influence of women, (4) environmental vulnerability and awareness, (5) matter and energy discoveries, (6) the rise of computer culture, (9) the startling decline in Western society, and (8) the basic power shift in global politics.

Sorensen, Barbara. *'Tis a Gift to be Simple.* Minneapolis, Minn.: Augsburg Fortress, 1992.

Todaro, Michael P. *Economic Development in the Third World.* 4th Ed. New York: Longman, 1989. In-depth examination of developmental economics as a social science. Concerned with human beings and social systems, the book focuses on activities that satisfy basic material needs as well as nonmaterial wants. Besides examining the developing world, it explores international possibilities and prospects. There are several editions available, from 1977 to 2000.

Voran, Marilyn Helmuth. *Add Justice to Your Shopping List.* Scottdale, Pa.: Herald Press, 1986. Now out of print but an excellent short guide for reshaping your food-buying habits according to the reality of justice. Insightful comments on economics and supermarkets. Includes suggestions for making your own convenience foods.

White, William R. *Fatal Attractions.* Nashville, Tenn.: Abingdon Press, 1992.